TALES
of
HERMIT
UNCLE
JOHN

TALES
of
HERMIT
UNCLE
JOHN

Roger
Robbennolt

Forest of
Peace Books

Also by the Author:
(available from Forest of Peace Books)

Tales of Gletha, the Goatlady

TALES OF HERMIT UNCLE JOHN

copyright © 1993, by Roger L. Robbennolt

Library of Congress Catalog Card Number: 92-83892
ISBN: 0-939516-17-9

published by
Forest of Peace Books, Inc.
PO Box 269
Leavenworth, KS 66048-0269 U.S.A.

printed by
Hall Directory, Inc.
Topeka, KS 66608

first printing: February 1993

cover art and illustrations by
Edward Hays

art consultation by
David DeRousseau

In Celebration of John Robbennolt
Herein Mythologized in Love

For Pat
The mystery of their love saved the boy
The mystery of your love saves the man

With Gratitude
To the community of Shantivanam
for keeping the Sacred Story flowing

A WORD FROM THE AUTHOR

A vision has shaped itself in my heart. It deals with finding a place of refuge for the hurting child which walks within each of us.

That vision first found expression in *Tales of Gletha, the Goatlady*. The figure of power is an outcast woman deeply in touch with those healing springs which flow from the heart of creation and which cleanse the boy Roger from despair.

In this collection, *Tales of Hermit Uncle John*, a war-shattered old man leads the battered boy into the wonderworld of hope enriched by practical ethical dimensions.

The themes of these books emerge in spite of the author whose only real intent has been to shape good stories in which the writing is undergirded by the sonorities of the Storyteller's voice.

To my amazement, these tales of the heart find their way into therapists' offices to use with clients, into classrooms as reading texts, into church study groups and in a hundred other unexpected places.

May you encounter joy and healing tears and a deep-running sense that you are not alone.

TABLE OF CONTENTS

A PROLOGUE AND A PARTING

The stock truck pulled up to the door of our northern Minnesota shack. The odor of every steer it'd ever hauled overpowered the scent of the surrounding pines.

Dirk Aaronsen directed the crew of neighboring pulpwood cutters as they carried out the meager furnishings and placed them in the front of the slatted bed.

I fled sobbing through the forest and across the intervening fields to my only place of refuge: the shack of Gletha, the goatlady. I needed a final good-bye touch.

Through the times of stark brutality I was subjected to by my mentally ill father as he sank into his "darknesses," the outcast woman would veil me in her soft grey cloths—indistinguishable as articles of clothing—with which she draped herself.

There I discovered a tent of meeting, a place of meaning. But that was soon to end. Weeks before, I had listened to the shouted musings of my father: "Mary, we're going to leave this god-forsaken place. I can't stand it any longer. We're goin' back where there are open fields of good soil that will actually grow something."

My mother had responded quietly: "Frank, you thought you'd be better up here where you'd be able to hunt and fish. You can work in the woods to make a little money to live on.

And I know folks here. Besides, the boy is as happy as he can be under the circumstances."

My father flared again: "That's one of the reasons we're movin'. I want to get the kid out from under the spell of that damned old witchwoman. I want my son ag'in."

She shot back, "You'll never really have either one of us if you can't somehow keep from sinking into your mind's darkness. I...."

Her sentence was destroyed by the sound of a slashing slap. She cried out in pain. The screen door slammed, and she ran sobbing into the night. I heard her running up the path to the two-seater toilet deep in the hazelnut bushes. She would hook the door on the inside in case my father pursued her.

I buried my head beneath my pillow. I was overcome by a sense of impending loss.

At the moment, however, I was swathed in the security of the gossamer fabric and the warm pressure of Gletha's enfolding arms. The familiar incense of the goatshed soothed me.

"G-G-Gletha, I c-c-can't st-st-stand to leave you. Where w-w-will I go when he hurts me b-bad?"

She pushed me firmly into a ladder-back chair at the kitchen table and moved around to the other side. She stared at me for a long moment. She held me in the intensity of those pools of darkness which were her eyes.

Then she spoke: "Boy, you don't learn so good, do you? How many times do I have to tell you that lovin' and bein' with have nothing to do with geography. All you gotta' do is remember all the times we've touched. The healin' will go on.

"And maybe what I've meant to you will appear in somebody else in her or his own way. And whenever you're touched in that way, all the love you've ever had will come wellin' up and hug your heart. But you've got to reach out for it and let it come and savor it while you got it."

I leaped from the chair and ran around the table. She held up a forbidding hand.

"We're not gonna' touch no more. You're gonna' begin practicin' right now. We each know that we carry the other in a special place. We can walk away and still be together."

The firm edge of her voice disquieted me. I began to back away, my eyes not leaving hers. I neared the door. She began to sing one of her strange forest songs. My heart lifted. I walked through the door and heard in the distance the answering song of a loon.

I dragged across the field. The grazing deer paid me no attention. I paused to watch a nursing fawn. Its weak twin had been mercifully brought down and devoured by timber wolves. I no longer had to watch it unable to nurse, teetering on its spindly legs at the edge of death.

The doe turned her large eyes toward me. She seemed to sense my pain. She butted away the remaining fawn, gorged with milk. She turned her side in such a way as if to invite me to refresh myself from her half-spent udder. In spite of myself, I laughed.

Returning through the hazelnut bushes, I heard sobs coming from the outhouse. I called out softly, "You okay, Mom?"

"I'm just real sad about leavin'. Step in here and give me a hand. I'm decent."

I entered cautiously. I was somewhat embarrassed. I hoped nobody saw me. When my eyes adjusted to the darkness of the dank shack, I saw on the seat beside her a stack of her beautiful crocheting. It was what she did to assure herself that she was real in the face of my father's terror.

"Wh-Wh-Why did you bring those th-things out to the toilet?"

"Yer dad said that I couldn't clutter up the inside of the car with my things. I couldn't stand the thought of all of 'em smelling of cow dung for the next twenty years. I decided to wrap them so they wouldn't absorb the odor."

She was wrapping each doily and tablecloth in pages of the out-of-date Montgomery Ward catalogue found in every outhouse in Bear Run Township and beyond.

The forest peace was torn by the squawk of a car horn followed by a bellow from my father: "You two git yer butts into this car or I'm goin' off without you."

I thought for a moment and said, "L-L-Let him g-g-go. We c-can make it."

My mom replied, "There's no way I can leave him or be left. We're together. Sometimes."

We headed out of the shack, our arms loaded, toward an uncertain future. We slipped up to the loaded truck.

She told me, "Climb over the side of the truck. See if you can git to a bureau drawer. I'll hand my things up to you."

I did as I was instructed. Then I scrambled down quickly.

The car horn sounded again. Dad was driving slowly down the driveway as if to desert us forever. In my heart's ear, the horn did not drown out the atonal hymn of the loon.

THE MEETING

The thorns on the gooseberry bushes tore at my bare limbs. My forehead was ripped by a dry, knife-like protrusion. I had tripped over a dead branch and fallen face-forward into the brambles. I sensed the supple stalks close over me.

I lay motionless. The pain from my scratched extremities was mild compared to the whip's slashes down my back. My lungs were raw from a two-mile run through patterns of brush and open fields. I lay absolutely still. He would never find me here.

His last words burned into my memory: "Don't you ever try to run away from me ag'in, you no-good little bastard! I'll find you wherever you hide."

Having finished the beating, my father bent over me. He cracked the horsewhip in his hand as I crouched naked and tearless in the urine-soaked straw of the horsebarn stall. I watched his hunched, shadowed figure turn and disappear into the light through the barn's double doors. I waited for a few moments. I pulled on my bib overalls and scuttled through a hole in the opposite wall of the half-ruined building.

We had just moved to this burned-out farm. I knew no one. My mother had sworn me to secrecy about the fact that my daddy was sick in the head. We'd continue to hide him when he was at his worst. My eleven-year-old body was shattered once more. I turned and ran as fast as I could in the opposite direction from his grim leave-taking.

A slight movement brought me back to my brambled predicament. A huge black beetle crawled down a twig to a dangling, fat, ripe berry which immediately began to twirl. The insect rode it like a circus aerialist. The stem gave way. Berry and beast fell to the soil a few inches from my nostrils. The beetle kicked helplessly as it landed on its back. Then it lay still.

For a moment I felt at one with the beetle. I didn't want to move for fear of betraying my hiding place to a possibly pursuing father. Feeling the terrible discomfort of my own position, I decided there was no need for both boy and bug to suffer. I imperceptibly moved my right hand toward the insect which now glowed almost purple in the shaft of sunlight illumining us both. The berry thorns scratched more deeply into the tender flesh of my underarm. I felt somehow disengaged from the hand which resembled a gigantic crab as fingers pulled it toward my stricken cohort. Thumb and forefinger surrounded the purple-black object.

Its legs had begun to wave aimlessly in the air once more. The legs never stopped. The moment the now-righted creature touched the earth, it lumbered off. It, at least, was free.

The shaft of hot August sunlight bore in more intently upon the berry patch. Perspiration ran down my back, further inflaming the lash marks and the bramble scratches. At last I felt free to cry. The first tear fell to the ground. Before being absorbed into the dust, it gathered to its surface a sheen of pollen. Then it disappeared, leaving only a black dot on the dry, grey surface.

The sunlight was cut off. I felt rather than heard a footstep near me. I tensed my body, waiting to be discovered by my searching father. The gooseberry brambles would be torn away. The sharp whistle of the descending whip would assault my ears before its tip gashed me once more.

Instead, I felt something cold and moist exploring the arch

of my bare left foot. A soft voice betraying a worse stammer than my own mused softly: "Wh-Wh-Why, T-T-Tiny, l-look at that. Th-th-those gooseberries c-caught themselves a p-p-prize. I d-d-don't know if it's a d-dwarf or an elf or a b-b-boy." The gooseberry bushes gently parted. I saw a kneeling figure which looked as if it were folded in upon itself. The resemblance to my father was unmistakable. It had to be my Hermit Uncle John.

I'd heard about my Uncle John all my life. I'd been told that he *had been* six-foot-four. I was told that he'd *had* a wonderful singing voice. He could sing a robin off a branch. I was told that he had *once* been able to listen to anybody—and listen deep. Everybody told him about their darkness and their light.

His laugh could be heard a mile away. When harvest time rolled around everybody wanted my Uncle John on their threshing crews. He'd work from sunup to harvest moon and keep all the workers happy.

I was told that he *once* loved to dance—that he could dance all night to the music of Fiddler Tom. I was told that he was the gentlest man in the whole wide world. I was also told that he was handsome. Every unmarried lady in Sunrise Township had had her heart set on marrying my Uncle John.

Then my Uncle John marched off to fight in one of those wars to end all wars: World War I. He never was touched by an enemy bullet, but something terrible happened to him in the worst place of all—inside himself.

He experienced stark terror at the Battle of the Marne. His entire company was killed—all except him. When the attack was over, he fought his way through the barbed wire and the mud interlaced with bits of his buddies' bodies.

He was given a medical discharge for whatever it was that went wrong in his mind. He returned to Sunrise Township. Folk didn't recognize him at first. He was all bent over. There was terror in his eyes. He couldn't stand to look at anybody. No longer did he lead out in the singing and the laughing. He'd developed a terrible stammer.

He learned he couldn't stand being around people. He moved to a little shack way back in the woods on the shore of Lake Sumach. Some of his family had lived there off and on for eighty years. His few needs were met by an army pension.

Sometimes he'd slip out at night to get flour and sugar and coffee at Kahler's Korner Kountry Store. If folk from around there saw him, they'd comment, "There goes old, dumb John." Coming home in the moonlight, his cheeks would be stained with tears.

Now and then he'd hear their comments and pretend not to. If folk who remembered him as he once had been tried to talk to him, he'd work to stammer out a word. Most often, he'd quietly disappear. Until I appeared, the terror had walled off the caring listener inside him.

He stammered some further comments to Tiny. She'd finished the exploration of my feet and now had burrowed beneath the brambles and begun work on my left ear. "It's a b-b-boy all right—though I was really rather hoping it might be one of those m-m-mythological creatures."

He chuckled as he folded his arms around me and lifted my slight body from its bramble-barred green prison. The pressure of his arms caused a gentle torment to flow across my back. Beneath the pain there was a kind of affirmation.

He shifted me so that I curled around his shoulders. I remembered the stained glass window in the Lakeside Church of Jesus Risen. Jesus, the Good Shepherd, carried a lamb around *his* shoulders. At that moment, I knew the lamb's security.

He stammered, "What's y-y-your name, boy?"

I stammered back, "R-R-Roger."

"My God, you must be Frank's b-b-boy. I've scarcely seen them since they adopted you. I heard th-th-that you were moving back from the northern parts. It s-seems strange not to recognize my own n-n-nephew."

He set me down on a path overarched with walnut trees. Tiny scampered ahead. Standing behind me, he pulled the straps of my too-large overalls and looked down my still-bleeding back. "That was not all c-c-caused by gooseberry stickers. What happened to you, b-b-boy?"

I wanted desperately to tell him, but my mother's fear of anybody finding out and causing us "terrible embarrassment" overcame me. I could only respond, "N-N-Nothing, sir. I fell on s-s-something."

"The last th-th-thing in the world I want any nephew of mine to do is l-l-lie. No simple f-fall would m-m-make marks like that."

Each comment he made seemed to take endless time as he stammered out his concern. He folded himself down on one knee. His warm brown eyes were on a level with mine. There were tears in them. He grabbed the back of my head and brought my face to a soft place between his chin and his shoulder. Through my perspiration-soaked hair I could feel the scratch of a two-day growth of whiskers. He held me there in a grip I wanted to last forever. I cried softly. The pain lessened.

He continued, "Frank's still moving into what your Mom always called his 'd-d-darknesses.' There's never been anything anybody could do. That's where the l-l-lash marks came from. Right? He's in another d-d-darkness."

"I ain't supposed t-t-to say."

"You don't have to *say* n-n-nothing. With the trouble we b-b-both have getting w-w-words out, we'll say as l-l-little as p-possible. Let's just follow Tiny up the path."

He took hold of my hand. It was lost inside his enormous fist. He seemed to hunger for continued touch as much as I.

The sun was setting as we stepped into a little clearing. On the far side a raggedy looking shack leaned against a granite outcropping known in the neighborhood as Shaman's Point. It looked as if it had grown, mushroom-like, out of the rock itself. In the red glow of the sun's farewell rays it resembled the witch's house in my fifth-grade reader's version of *Hansel and Gretel*. I glanced out of the corner of my eye at the crabbed figure by my side. The tenderness of his giant touch on my hand made me feel that the shack's gnome-like occupant was, for the moment, benevolent.

It was then that I became aware of the odor: a cinnamony, sweet-tart smell of cooking fruit leavened by the additional aroma of browning pastry.

"I'll l-l-leave you here with T-T-Tiny for a minute. I was m-m-making myself a gooseberry pie. I'll g-g-get it out of the oven so it can cool down a bit. Maybe I'll even share a piece with you before I s-s-send you home."

He gave my hand a squeeze, dropped it and disappeared into the shack. As the screen door slammed behind him, I was suddenly aware of being bone shatteringly tired. I sank into the lush grass. Tiny twined herself around my bare feet and descended into body jerking, rabbit chasing dreams. My angry father receded further into space and time.

Returning, my Hermit Uncle John proposed, "While the pie cools, we'd better clean you up a bit."

I grasped his extended hand. As he pulled me to my feet, Tiny growled at being jostled. He gently nudged her away with his toe. She awakened immediately and grabbed his boot lace in her teeth, ready for an obviously familiar game.

"L-Later Tiny. We have other f-f-fish to fry at the moment."

Together, they led me around the corner of the shack which, from a distance, had seemed engulfed in brush. A smaller clearing had been hacked out of the tree-shadowed undergrowth. On one side the great rock rose up. The perimeter was edged with a profusion of yellow iris which seemed to retain the sun's rays in the gathering twilight. The air was filled with their sweet perfume. Within the enclosure I felt safely isolated from the whole world.

Near the corner of the house stood a cast-iron pump. At its side was a huge, round oak tub. Colonies of lush green moss decorated its sides. It was full of water. The pale image of a full moon was reflected on its surface.

Uncle John explained, "I f-f-filled the tub this morning so

the sun could warm it and I c-c-could have a good, long soak t-t-tonight. I guess I could see my way clear to letting you use it first."

"But," I protested, "it's n-n-not even Saturday yet. Folks take their b-baths on S-S-Saturday—always."

"I never have b-b-been much for doing what other folks do when they do it. Now, g-g-get out of those overalls and into the water."

I turned my back to him, slipped quickly out of my bib overalls and carefully covered my privates with my hands. In that moment I could almost feel my father's sharp, painful slap on my face when I'd failed to perform that gesture of modesty in his presence. His attendant voice knifed through my memory, "Don't ever let me see you naked ag'in without your covering your shame."

I turned toward the tub and realized that I couldn't step over its high edge without using my hands for balance. I paused in confusion.

Uncle John looked at me, a half-smile illumining his lined face. He said quietly, "Son, you d-d-don't have to keep your p-p-penis and testicles covered up. Hasn't anybody ever t-told you that the human body is b-b-beautiful when it's not used to destroy itself or anybody else?"

I was amazed. Gletha was the only one who ever called my body beautiful, and this was the first time I'd ever heard my privates called by their rightful names. He took my elbow and propelled me toward the tub. I removed my hands to the oaken edge and lowered myself into the sun-warmed depths. An indescribable sense of well-being flooded over me with the healing touch of water.

He handed me a rough-shaped white bar of soap. It smelled of wintergreen. I figured that any man who could make a gooseberry pie probably would have made the soap as well. I stood up and lathered as much of myself as I could reach. Uncle John took the soap and lathered my back, avoiding as best he could the worst of the lash welts.

He lathered my hair and then gently massaged my scalp. He turned and picked up a large battered white and grey abalone shell from the edge of the iris. He filled it with water and poured it slowly through my hair. It cascaded down my body. I felt every tortured muscle begin to relax.

A whippoorwill called in the distance. I was for a moment transported beyond my pain toward something like hope. I allowed myself to sink again into the water. I watched the patterns of soap on the surface obscure the reflected moon.

"You'd b-b-better come out, boy. We've got some other business to attend to before we g-g-get to the pie."

I stepped out of the tub. Tiny was ready for me. She began licking my ankle. It tickled. I broke into laughter as Uncle John engulfed me with the huge, soft old Turkish towel. He took me in his arms and hugged me dry.

Untwining the towel, he spread it out on the soft grass. "Stretch out on your t-t-tummy, son. Let's see what we can d-d-do for those welts."

I stretched out on the great soft towel, its damp coolness absorbed by the sun-warmed grass beneath. I heard my uncle unscrew the lid of a pint mason jar.

He explained: "I'll gently r-r-rub in this elixir of witch hazel. I boiled it up myself. It will st-st-sting a bit at first, but the whip marks and b-b-bramble scratches will feel a lot better."

His touch on my body was infinitely soft. The scent of the witch hazel elixir joined the perfume of the iris on the night air.

As his fingers flowed across my flesh, Uncle John whispered to himself: "I can't believe my own flesh-and-blood would do this to a b-b-boy. It would be b-bad enough to do it to a horse—but to living, human flesh and blood! I kn-kn-know he's ashamed at not being able to father a child of his own and having to adopt one. But he treats his stray d-d-dogs better. I've never been able to talk to him—sick or well. If I c-c-can't do nothing to help the m-m-man, maybe I c-can do something for the boy."

His fingers quivered. I heard his breath catch. Points of flame erupted on my back where his salt tears touched the unhealed wounds.

Finally he said, "Now, c-c-carefully r-r-roll over on your b-b-back. It won't hurt as bad now."

I rolled over. The damp towel had captured the warmth from the sun-heated earth. As the witch hazel and the moisture intermingled, the pain seemed drawn into the ground.

I stretched luxuriously as Uncle John stroked the elixir along my arms, across my chest and stomach, down my legs and finally up my neck and into my bramble-scratched cheeks. Every muscle relaxed. I somehow felt all together in one piece. I had no compulsion to "hide my shame."

Uncle John stammered out in a half-whisper, "You sure look l-l-like you feel a lot better than when I found you. Sit up real slow now, or you'll f-f-fall on your face."

I rose. My body felt the lead weight of total relaxation. Uncle John picked up the abalone shell, pumped it full of water and poured the ice-cold fluid over me. I screeched—but felt considerably enlivened. He grabbed a second towel and hugged me dry a final time. A sense of contentment flowed over his loneliness-shattered face.

He handed me my overalls. I slipped into them while savoring the moments of naked freedom with which my Hermit Uncle John had gifted me.

I was unbelievably hungry. "I-I-Is it gooseberry pie time yet?" I asked hopefully, breathing in the last traces of cinnamon on the evening air.

He looked at the palette of the sky overhead, painted with the final rays of the setting sun and the rising moon. He responded, "I think we have one more stop to make before we head pieward. It's always my last stop before going inside for the evening."

I hoped the stop would be brief.

Tiny, knowing well this end-of-day routine, headed around the end of the rock wall at the cabinside. We followed her behind the corner of the great granite outcropping and up a steep path. We stepped out onto a flat surface. I gasped. It was as if we were floating in space.

Above us sunrays and moonrays were interlocked. Stars were struggling to become visible. To the east the great pale yellow globe of the full harvest moon was lazily emerging above the oak trees and the distant fields of ripening oats and barley broken by rich, green squares of corn.

To the west the dying fire of the day slowly faded, making a crimson backdrop for a long vee of Canadian honkers hymning their way north.

Below us, almost as far as the eye could see, the darkening waters of Lake Sumach stretched toward the west. Final touches of the sun's fire caught the night breeze's ripples. To the east headlights crawled along the roadway. Some of them paused at Kahler's Korner. From our vantage point a ramshackle collection of roofs—various sizes of squares and oblongs—clustered along one side of a great, round central hall like piglets to a nursing sow. The collection was fronted by a large, illuminated sign informing passersby that herein could be found "GROCERIES, COLD BEER, WORMS, POOL, BAR AND GRILL, DANCING."

Directly across the lake stood a small, white church. The surrounding woods seemed to be trying to push it off the granite ledge on which it was built and into the water below. A brave little steeple pleaded with the heavens. As if in answer an angry red star glowered fiercely on its very tip. The fading yellows of the sunset flamed in its windows.

"Uncle J-J-John, what's the star at the t-t-tip of that church steeple?" I queried.

"It's the planet Mars."

Having learned my ancient myths well, I said proudly, "It's n-n-named for the god of war."

"You d-d-don't say! W-Well, it sure is sitting in the right p-p-place. The folk in the Baptist Church of Peter-the-Rock always seem to be trying to d-d-destroy each other."

"Do you ever g-g-go to church over there?" I asked.

"They don't want the likes of me around them. Th-th-they've made that real clear. So I just c-c-come up here every night."

The night breeze chilled me. I seemed to grow taller as it grew darker. If I stretched out my arm, I could twirl a star on my fingertip or maybe even shake hands with God.

"Uncle J-J-John, why do you come up here?"

"I g-g-guess maybe something draws me here. Your great-grandfather built a house right there where m-m-mine is now. He wrote a letter to his sister back in Pennsylvania telling her that he'd heard that this gr-great rock and all the land surrounding it was holy gr-gr-ground to the Sioux Indians. Their shamans w-w-would come right to this very rock and light their sacred f-f-fires. Young boys would wait h-h-here for a vision. Old men would come to die. Pregnant women would stand here to assure strength for their b-b-babies.

"One day your great-grandfather came back from a trip and found the Indians had burned his cabin. He rebuilt, and he married your great-grandmother. Together they had my daddy, Anton, who was also your daddy's daddy.

"On an April morning y-y-your gr-gr-great-grandmother carried baby Anton across the fields to visit a neighbor. The Sioux came riding through here on one of the l-l-last uprisings this country ever knew. They killed your great-grandfather and thirty-two other folks and threw their bodies in Massacre Slough. S-S-Somehow, they missed the f-farmstead where his w-w-wife and baby were.

"Some Indians were c-c-caught and accused of the k-k-killings. They were taken to Fort Snelling and hanged. Folks always said their spirits came back here to the rock to wait for a time when they could reclaim their holy p-p-place. Some folk even say that there are nights when a mysterious red fire burns r-r-right here where we're standing.

"I've always felt s-s-sorry for the Sioux. We stole their land. I just come up here every night and join them. They don't make fun of how I talk or look. The longer I'm up here with my unseen friends, the less I stammer."

The fingers of the breeze caressed me like unseen hands curiously exploring a newcomer. Tiny let out a mournful howl. I nearly jumped out of my skin!

In my fear I queried, "Uncle J-J-John, isn't it about pie time?"

He laughed quietly. "I got so involved in the story I forgot the pie."

The Church of Peter-the-Rock had faded into the darkness leaving Mars to glower in lonely splendor. Tiny led the way down. As he turned to go, Uncle John murmured something under his breath. It sounded like, "Good night, good friends." There was not a trace of a stammer.

As we approached the door of the ancient shack, the old man struck a match. He lit a kerosene lantern which hung inside a tiny porch that shielded the front door. As we entered, he busied himself lighting three lamps mounted on the walls of a large center room. He was so bent over that he carried with him a three-step, rough wrought wooden stool. The lamps in our house were often smoky. The globes of these were polished as if they were rare crystal. The metal reflectors behind them imaged the opposite walls like the finely-silvered surfaces of royal mirrors.

He stepped into the little kitchen. Tiny had already curled up in a corner box lined with soft straw. Her limbs were moving, and there was an occasional soft "yip" as she again chased rabbits in her sleep.

From the kitchen I heard the familiar clang of a cast-iron skillet on the lid of the wood burning cookstove. Soon the shack was filled with the rich smell of frying fish.

I was left to wonder at the magic grotto in which I found myself. Every inch of the floor beneath my bare feet was covered with woven straw mats. The walls were tapestried with intricately crafted reed mats patterned with the rich brown heads of cattails and various kinds of nuts. Running across every wall around the room was a fine design which caught the lamplight. I looked closer and found that it was made up of hundreds of arrowheads.

Three wooden shelves were set into a corner. They were filled with small decorated clay pots and broken pieces with strange birds and animals on them. I realized that designs from the pottery were repeated endlessly in the wall hangings.

On the opposite side of the room beneath the largest of the lamps stood a small shelf containing seven books with matching bindings. They were within easy reach of a well-worn easy chair. I knelt down to see their titles embossed in gold on fine leather: *The Complete Tales of the Brothers Grimm*, *The Complete Tales of Hans Christian Andersen*, *The Complete Fables of Aesop*, *The Complete Works of William Shakespeare*, *The History of the Decline and Fall of the Roman Empire* by Edward Gibbon, *The Religion of the Red Man* by Ernest Thompson Seton and *The Holy Bible*.

Uncle John came into the room and set two each of plates and glasses and knives and forks on a small straw-matted table.

As he turned I asked, "Where did you get all these beautiful b-b-books?"

"I b-b-bought the whole set from a peddler before I went off to war. Th-Th-Then I got them only because I thought they were beautiful. Now I'm sure they contain just about everything a person ever needs to know."

Having once been called a "little walking Bible" after the great Bible verse memorization contest at the Lakeside Church of Jesus Risen, I asked Uncle John what he thought about *The Holy Bible* and how it was different from the other books on his shelf.

He was silent for a moment. Then he responded, "S-S-Some folks say it was written by God. I think it was more apt to have been wr-wr-written by people like us who came down off r-r-rocks, just like we did a few minutes ago, where they knew they were in special touch with something holy. Then they told stories about wh-wh-what they saw or heard or felt.

"Later on by firelight or oil lamplight or candlelight they wrote the st-st-stories down. I've always been sorry they ever wrote them. If the stories had continued to be t-t-told, maybe they'd have been lived better. But it's a fine book, and you can never understand it too well. Trouble is, you can't just r-r-read it with your head. You've got to r-r-read it with your heart for it to come alive in your life.

"But that's enough questions for now. Sit yourself down at the table. Let's eat."

Just as I was about to seat myself on the ladder-back chair across from my uncle, I felt something soft and furry slither from beneath me. Glancing at the floor, I saw a small black and white skunk staring up at me.

I cried out, "Uncle John, we got to g-g-get outta' here. There's a sk-sk-skunk in the room. It'll ruin everything."

He laughed: "I should have warned you. That's only old Pity Me. She's been fixed so she can't shoot her protective scent. She's been a good friend."

He bent over and picked up the little animal as if it were a pussy cat.

"She's a rather unusual skunk. She's got four narrow alternating black and white bands down her face. Most skunks have got two. You never know what you might notice if you really look at the world close. You also never know how valuable such a close look might be."

He carried the skunk across the room and put her on the floor.

He said, "Now: call her just the way you'd call a cat. Say, 'Here, kitty, kitty!' "

I tentatively called, "Here, kitty, kitty."

Pity Me dashed across the floor and climbed into my lap. I stroked her ears. Tiny, awakened by the smell of food, pulled jealously at my pant leg while Uncle John went chuckling to the kitchen.

He brought in a hobnailed glass pitcher of milk and a high-risen loaf of bread with the slicing knife balanced halfway through the initial piece. As he passed slowly by a lamp, the far wall was transformed by the enormous shadow of the bread and the pitcher and the shattered old man. Gletha had read to me the Bible story about the Last Supper. She told me how we were supposed to be in touch with Jesus whenever we sat at table, how the risen Christ was with us in a special way in the flesh of folk who really knew the meaning of love. I shivered. This first supper with my Hermit Uncle John was feeling something like I imagined that Last Supper felt to those who gathered around that distant table.

Returning to the kitchen, he reemerged with a majestic platter of fried fish. As he placed it on the table and seated himself, I reached for my fork. His great hand engulfed mine.

"I always like to s-s-savor in silence the fact that there's food on the table before I savor the food itself—particularly since this food comes from sacred ground and sacred water. And besides, this is a special time. It's the first occasion in the twenty-five years I've lived here th-th-that anyone visible has j-j-joined me for a meal."

He closed his eyes and I closed mine. A strange energy flowed through our touching hands. I realized that inside the shack he scarcely stammered. Neither did I. I wondered if some of the good friends from the rock hadn't joined us around the table.

My reverie was broken by the removal of his hand. He forked four fat bullheads from the fish platter to my plate. They were crisply wrapped in a golden covering of cornmeal. The fish were followed by a thick slice of the lightest bread I'd ever eaten. It must have been baked immediately before the pie. I spread it with sweet butter while Uncle John filled my glass with milk which still carried a hint of warmth from the cow's udder.

For some time we ate in silence, broken only by Tiny's occasional begging "woofs." My curiosity got the best of me.

"Uncle John, where did the pots and the pieces on your shelves come from?"

"From my garden. Every time I dig in it to make it a little bigger, I'm liable to unearth a small pot or a broken piece. Sometimes a little container will be filled with arrowheads—though I'm always finding them scattered through the woods.

"Strange things from far away turn up, like the abalone shell in the iris garden. Once in a while I find a human bone—sometimes a skull. Occasionally the skull is split in such a way that I suspect the person's been tomahawked. I found one the other day with a p-p-pair of holes shattered through front and back. That one'd probably been shot."

I wasn't sure I'd ever want to help my Hermit Uncle John dig in his garden.

I asked, "What do you do with the bones—just stick 'em back in the ground?"

"I take them up to the tip of the rock. I leave them so they can know some freedom in the wind and the rain and the moon and the sun and the stars. At dawn I return them to the earth beneath a huge, old sprawling oak tree.

"A medicine show once stopped at Kahler's Korner before I went to war. An Indian was dancing in the show before the magic cure-alls were sold. He came out and sat for a while under that tree. He said he'd been brought here as a child and been taught the special ceremonies and dances. He had become a shaman. He said that he needed to come back regularly. Sometimes I think he does and I don't see him. We got along real good."

During the course of the story four more fish appeared on my plate, my glass was refilled and further slices of bread were cut. My Uncle John buttered one slice specially for me and sprinkled a little sugar on it. A preacher in Vacation Bible School had told us about the manna in the wilderness. I guessed I was probably eating something similar now.

The voracious edge of my appetite appeased, my eyes strayed to the kitchen door to see if I could spot the initial reason for our coming inside.

Uncle John chuckled. The sound was a bit raspy, as if he

were out of practice.

"Help me clear these things away. Then I'll see what else I c-c-can find. "

As I rose to carry our plates into the tiny kitchen, Pity Me slithered off my lap and headed for the soft cushions of Uncle John's reading chair. A gigantic cookstove filled most of the space. Drying herbs hung from the rafters above. A kitchen cabinet with a flour bin, bread drawer and space for a few dishes, spices and cooking utensils occupied the opposite wall. A long counter held a water bucket, washbasin, dishpan and rinsepan. I put our supper things in the dishpan. Uncle John covered them with warm water from the reservoir built into the side of the cookstove.

"All right, boy. Take your seat. I'll bring it in. "

He stepped through the rear door of the kitchen. I peeked around the corner and saw him pick up the pie from the porch railing where it had been placed to cool. I raced for my chair.

He bore it to the table like a wizened priest transporting a sacramental offering to the altar. It glowed in the lamplight like burnished gold. It sparkled from the coarse sugar sprinkled on the top. The crust's castellated edge was as even as that on a crown for a young prince. The steam-release prickings on the over-crust were patterned like a picture from one of the grave pots. I knew our good friends from the rock were pleased.

He cut a quarter of the pie and put it in a flat bowl. He poured thick, rich cream over the delicacy and placed it in front of me. I was awestruck. I put a tiny piece in my mouth. The gooseberries had not cooked to mush. They popped as I bit carefully into them, releasing their sweet-tartness into the surrounding cinnamon syrup. The crust had retained a tender crispness.

He chuckled again. The sound was smoother this time.

"The expression on your f-f-face makes the work worth it. "

I felt claws scraping down the leg of my overalls. I looked below the table edge. At my notice, Tiny put her paws imploringly on my knee.

Uncle John quickly clarified the situation for me. "I'm sorry. I forgot to instruct you in the most important rule of the household. We do not ever eat the raised edge of crust. Tiny looks upon that as her private property."

I reluctantly broke off the succulent pastry and extended it to the salivating dog. To my amazement she took it daintily in her mouth, trotted across the floor and laid it in her bed. She then returned to her master's side. He had already broken off his crust. Before taking the offering, she licked his hand. Returning to her nest of straw, she nibbled at the morsels as if wanting them to last as long as possible.

Having finished the pie, I felt my eyelids getting heavy. Uncle John said, "I think it's t-t-time to get you home. Your mother will worry about you."

"It's okay. I often r-r-run away and hide when Dad's in one of his d-d-darknesses."

Tears again sprang to his eyes.

"At least you'd better go home for her. I'll walk you part of the way."

We cleared the table. As a delaying tactic, I even offered to dry the dishes. He remained firm.

Tiny raced through the door ahead of us. She immediately treed a fat raccoon. The masked beast stared at us from a low limb as we passed in the light of the full moon.

We crossed the oat stubble of a nearby field. I looked back at the upper reaches of Shaman's Point outlined against the night sky. Was there not the red glow of a fire backed by the profusion of light which was the Milky Way?

The hair caterpillared on the back of my neck. I felt a surge of fear all the way to my toes. I tugged at the sleeve of my Uncle John's faded blue chambray shirt and pointed wordlessly.

He looked and then quietly responded, "D-D-Don't even ask any questions, Roger."

"But don't you get scared living right underneath whatever is there?"

He thought for a moment as we walked on. Then he responded, "N-N-No. I'm not af-f-fraid. I've l-l-lived with the m-m-mystery so long it's become a friend."

He took my hand and we walked a long way in silence through groves of oaks and maples. We crossed open fields and balanced on fallen trees across little rivulets.

We arrived at the south edge of the field which fronted our small frame house. In the distance I could see a dim light in the window. Uncle John knelt at my side and took me in his arms. Holding me close he stammered out, "If y-y-you ever need me, you know you can always c-c-come. If you n-n-need me and can't c-c-come, just think of me d-deeply. Something of me will be with you. We've been to the t-t-top of the rock together."

He rose, turned abruptly and walked off the way we'd come. Before descending out of sight into a little gully, he turned and waved to me. Then he disappeared.

I walked slowly across the field, not knowing what I would find when I stepped through the door. I turned and took one last look at the full moon, the Milky Way and glowering Mars. I wished I could see from here the red glow at the tip of the great rock.

I opened the screen door softly, passed through the kitchen and looked into the small living room. My father was sitting motionless in his favorite creaky rocking chair, his head in his hands, his elbows resting on his knees, deep in one of his darknesses. My mother sat by the single kerosene lamp. She would have gladly washed its smoky globe, but Dad preferred the light to be dull and soft. She was crocheting one of her endless antimacassars which would ultimately decorate most of the living rooms in the neighborhood.

Hearing me, she raised her eyes from her work and placed a finger to her lips. I tiptoed over to her to give her an obligatory "good-night" peck on the cheek.

She whispered, "I'm afraid this is going to be one of his worst. Just keep away from him for a few days, and he'll get all right again."

She lifted her face. I saw a dark, fresh bruise on her cheek. I placed an unusually long, gentle kiss in its midst. I glanced at the almost-completed crocheted piece in her lap. Above the horns of a leaping stag appeared the words, "GOD BLESS OUR HAPPY HOME."

I tiptoed around my father and went into my bedroom. I lighted the little lamp on my bureau, determined that tomorrow I would polish its globe to resemble fine crystal. In the dim light I saw our three-legged black kitten curled up on my pillow. I unsnapped the bib on my overalls where I carried the worn yellow teddy bear I'd been given the Christmas when I was four, right after I'd been adopted. I took out the bear and placed it by the sleeping cat. The bear and I had been through six years of torment together.

I slipped out of my overalls and hung them on a peg in my cramped closet. Before donning my worn, nearly outgrown, homemade pajamas, I stepped in front of my bureau. I allowed my toes the luxury of curling up in the soft fur of the raccoonskin rug. I looked in the tall mirror. In the midst of the dark patches where the silvering had gone bad, I could see my body. It was good. I needn't be ashamed. A warm feeling suffused my loins. My penis swelled a bit in celebration.

I turned and looked at my back. The angry red whip welts had nearly disappeared.

Dear Gletha,

I'm sending this letter along with Mom's to Aunt Jennie Mauldin. I know she'll get it to you some way. As usual, there's not much money so I saved a stamp.

We got here okay. Skippy misses the pine woods, but there are patches of other kinds of woods around here so he still has squirrels and raccoons to chase.

Mom and I are scared. Dad promised he'd be all well if we moved south. He beat us again real bad. I ran away and was found by somebody who's a lot like you but different. He's my dad's youngest brother, John. He's a hermit and people laugh at him, but I always feel better when I'm with him. This may not be so bad after all.

I wasn't going to tell you about my Hermit Uncle John because I didn't want to hurt your feelings by finding another person to love, and then I thought you'd be sure to understand.

Some Canadian honkers passed over tonight. I was feeling lonely, but I thought maybe they'd pass your way too and we'd have heard the same song.

Love,

Rog

Dear Rogee,

Jennie gave me your note yesterday and says I can always tuck in one back with her letter. She plans to write to your mom real often.

I'm glad you found your Hermit Uncle John. Don't worry about me being jealous. Paul in the Bible sent a letter to some folk in Corinth and told them that real love is never jealous. I don't always agree with what he says, but I agree with that.

I just heard that we dropped a terrible bomb on Japan and that the war is about over. War will never be over till folks learn to share their hearts.

Each time a honker passes over I'll think of you. We've always been good at sharing songs.

Love,

Gletha

PITY ME

My mind whirled all night long. Though I had found a place of refuge from my daddy's anger, images of mysterious red fire and arrowheads and bits of bones now wove through my dreams. I kept waking up in fear as shadowy figures raised tomahawks above a fleeing boy. I was running toward the outstretched arms of my Hermit Uncle John. I never quite reached them before I awoke terrified.

I crept from my bed to relieve my aching kidneys. I didn't want to walk alone in the dark to the two-seater toilet at the edge of the grove behind the house. With my big toe I nudged Skippy, my mongrel dog, awake where he slept on a racoonskin rug. He growled and grabbed my bare ankle with mock ferocity. Then he followed me obediently up the well-worn path.

I stood in the dark shack relieving myself. I wondered if the old grey spider was centered in her corner-crossing web. Perhaps she had decided to explore the floor now occupied by my bare feet.

I leaped through the door! I almost landed on Skippy who lay with a stick in his mouth ready for a game. I grabbed it from his teeth and threw it as hard as I could. He tore after it. The movement called forth an atonal warning honk from Brutus, the great gander who guarded the chickenyard. Both dog and boy froze in their tracks, fearing an attack from that sharp-beaked predator who had often bruised them both.

The eastern sky glowed faintly with early morning light. The iron cock on the barn-top weather vane looked as if it had just crowed up the morning star which seemed to be balanced on its beak. The real roosters in the farmyard would soon begin their strident wake-up call.

I returned to the house. Skippy had disappeared. I hoped he was on the track of the weasel which had killed three of our best hens.

I wiped the dirt from my bare feet on the dew-soaked grass and stepped into the house. The rocking chair where my daddy always sat out his darknesses was empty. Mom had gotten him into bed last night. I closed the screen door quietly. I would not awaken him to screaming rage.

I made a decision. I had to revisit my Hermit Uncle John. The mysteries encountered the previous evening were too overwhelming to go unexplored.

I pulled on my overalls. I picked up my small yellow teddy bear who was partially hidden in my crumpled goosedown pillow. I unsnapped the giant bib pocket, folded the bear inside and resnapped his permanent daytime home.

I stood for a moment with my thumb nestling against the bear. He had become my constant companion when I was four. My folks had just taken me out of the orphanage. All the children who lived there shared a story. If you got taken by somebody before Christmas, there'd be stacks and stacks of presents. We knew whoever got us would be so tickled to have us that they would just bury us in gifts out of sheer gratitude.

Though evidence of my adoptive parents' poverty was everywhere, I still believed the story. On Christmas morning I dashed downstairs to the crookedy tree someone had given us just before the holy day. There was not a present in sight.

I collapsed in tears on the worn wood floor. Then, far back in the lower branches I saw him: the small yellow bear. I reached in and retrieved him. I immediately used him for what was to become his most important task during the next ten years: to dry my tears. Then I snapped him into my overall pocket for the first time.

When my daddy's violence overwhelmed me, I could always stay in touch with the bear until I found someone to hold me. Being under a promise to my mother to say nothing to anybody about Dad's mental illness, huggers were few and far between. When the kids on the playground ragged on me because of my stammer or my buck teeth, the bear was always there to comfort me.

I headed for the still-dark barnyard. I herded the reluctant cows into their stalls and secured their heads in the stanchions so they couldn't move around as I milked them. I wished that someone would invent rear hoof stanchions to prevent the more stubborn beasts from, on occasion, kicking over both pail of milk and milker.

I hunkered down on the three-legged stool next to old Betsy, the gentlest of the six animals who awaited my ministrations. I stroked her udder gently for a moment or two so that she would relax and "give down" her milk more fully.

Ghosting out of the darkness beneath a nearby manger came the black kitten. It had been born with three legs. Perhaps because of its handicap it was my favorite among the barnyard beasts.

As I milked, the kitten rubbed against my legs. Its *basso profundo* purr echoed up to the silent rafters where the sleeping pigeons were startled awake. It backed off a few paces and sat with its mouth open. Knowing that my father was nowhere around and wouldn't punish me for playing, I aimed a stream of milk from the cow's teat to the cat's mouth.

When I had finished my task, I carefully carried the pails of fresh milk to the back room off the kitchen where the cream separator was located. I set them on the floor where they would await my mother's evenhanded turning of the crank which resulted in the finest cream. I always turned the machine too fast or too slow.

I took a golden heel of bread from the kitchen cupboard, spread it thickly with butter and sprinkled it with sugar and cinnamon. I gobbled it down. I decided that would be enough food to last me until I once more could hopefully dine in splendor at the straw mat covered table in the shack by the holy lake.

I did my mother a favor before I left. I started a fire in the cookstove after carefully layering slivers of wood and dry corncobs. I set the coffee to boil. Perhaps she would be less prone to anger at my taking off so early in the morning.

I scrawled a note on a brown paper bag telling her where I was going. I left it by her place at the table.

I stepped into the tall alfalfa. My overall legs were instantly soaked, sending a cold shiver up my spine. The sun was just peeking up over the trees which lined Specter Slough to the east of our farm. I was glad for the encroaching light which would certainly be avoided by the ghost of Emma Ludwig for whom the slough was named.

Emma had been "tetched in the head"—or so the neighbors said. She wandered over the fields singing "Rescue the Perishing" in a high-pitched, off-key voice. She was a little, short woman. When she moved through a field of ripening oats, it looked like her head was floating level with the grain.

One night during harvest season she disappeared. A few days later her head was found in the shallow water of what was then called Jones Pond. The rest of her was never discovered.

Undertaker Turlew came up with a fine idea. Her folks bought an oak coffin carved with grapevines and lilies. He took a sheaf of oats and placed it in the coffin with the grain nestled around a mauve satin pillow on which he placed Emma's head.

Bettina Barsky who "did hair" for the undertaker commented to anyone who would listen that, "It was a real challenge to get the ringlets just right." Bettina hovered around the casket during visiting hours and made an occasional adjustment. She beamed with pleasure when viewers would comment, "Why, Bettina, Emma looks real natural."

Rev. Rory Rofstaedler, the new young preacher at Resurrection Baptist Church stumbled a bit during this, his first funeral service. He did emphasize that Emma, in particular, would rise a spiritual body. Not knowing the customs of the area, he was shocked when everybody brought their Kodak box cameras and took pictures of Emma and the oats before the lid was screwed down a final time.

Soon the story was passed around the township that when the harvest moon was full you could hear "Rescue the Perishing" echoing out of the muddy waters of what soon came to be renamed "Specter Slough." Mick McFadden swore he'd seen Emma's head perched on a shock of oats as he was on the way home from Pheasant Valley after having had only three beers.

I was a little worried when Skippy crouched on his haunches and directed a mournful howl toward the murky waters. Nothing untoward appeared.

The night birds and the guardians of the day were changing places. As the last vestiges of darkness flowed west before the reddening light, a barn owl flew over with a still-squeaking gopher in its claws, heading for its distant home. A great hawk rose out of a lightning-blasted oak and remained for a moment, silhouetted against the risen sun, hoping for similar prey.

Skippy flushed out pheasants and frightened mourning doves as he playfully scampered back and forth through fleeting patches of ground fog.

We were nearing the woods where the magic cabin nestled on the shore of the holy lake. Suddenly, I spotted a small black and white animal coming toward me. It was Pity Me, Uncle John's tame skunk. Skippy spotted the little creature. He turned tail and ran. He'd had disastrous encounters with skunks.

I decided to call Pity Me just as Uncle John had instructed me the previous evening. I would let the skunk ride on my shoulder as I walked to the cabin. My uncle would be so proud of me.

I knelt in the furrow and called, "Here, kitty, kitty, kitty. Here, kitty, kitty."

The little animal scampered toward me as it had the night before. Suddenly, six feet in front of me it turned, raised its tail and shot me with a burst of its vile-smelling protective perfume. I had made a terrible mistake. This skunk obviously was not Pity Me. The foreign beast scurried quickly away.

The spray burned my skin. My eyes were aflame. I was dizzy from the overwhelming odor.

I looked to Skippy for some kind of assistance. He was crouched in a distant furrow with his paws over his nose. I took a step toward him. He turned and ran for home as fast as he could.

I knew I was in real trouble. My Hermit Uncle John would have nothing to do with me smelling like this. I would never again have a place to go when my dad hurt me—and this time, he hadn't laid a hand on me.

Perhaps I could slip up to the tip of the granite outcropping. Maybe the wind would blow the odor away. However, that was a little scary. The whole world would smell the results of my error in identification.

Uncle John's invisible friends might work some special magic to rid me of my curse. On the other hand, they might just leave the rock forever.

I maundered along into the woods in a deep quandary. Tiny burst out of the bushes. She wanted me to play with her. She then discovered the source of the smell. She began to bark hysterically.

Pity Me was sunning herself on the doorstep. She looked at me intently for a moment, sniffed and slunk into the root cellar.

Uncle John stepped through the door, his *Holy Bible* in his hand, and started to greet me. He flared his nostrils and then stared in dumb amazement.

"I j-j-just been readin' about N-N-Noah placing burnt offerings on the altar and how the L-L-Lord smelled a sweet s-s-savor. All of a s-s-sudden I smelled s-something. I knew wh-wh-what I smelled would *not* have p-p-pleased the Lord. B-B-Boy, what h-h-happened to you?"

"I 'kitty-kittied' a skunk I was sure was P-P-Pity Me."

"H-How many st-st-stripes d-d-did that skunk have on its f-f-face?"

I responded miserably, "I d-d-didn't l-l-look close enough to see."

"Boy, you a-a-always g-got to look at the w-w-world careful-like, or you'll be in a h-h-heap of tr-trouble. Don't ever f-f-forget that. Always c-c-count the lines on the f-face of a skunk and the l-l-lines on the face of a person and the lines of the earth r-r-running through the forest. If you d-don't, you'll always be l-l-lost."

"Okay," I said, "s-s-so I'm lost. Wh-Wh-What do I d-do now?"

"W-W-Well, you best stay on the d-d-downwind side of me. St-St-Strip off those clothes and stretch out on your b-back under the pump spout. L-L-Let's take care of your eyes first."

I did as I was instructed. I smelled so bad and felt so sick that I didn't give my exposed privates a second thought. Uncle John dumped a can of water down the pump to prime it. At the same time he began moving the handle up and down.

Ice cold clear water poured over my face.

"F-F-Force yourself to keep y-your eyes open so that the water can f-f-flow across your eyeballs."

The stinging sensation began to go away. The smell, though overpowering still, had lessened.

"Now, th-th-throw your clothes in the oak t-tub and then g-g-get yourself in after them wh-wh-while I get something we n-n-need from the r-root cellar. L-Looks to me like I'm going to spend the r-r-rest of my l-l-life cleaning you up."

He disappeared into the storage area under the shack. I could hardly bring myself to touch the odoriferous overalls. I threw them in and climbed in after them.

Uncle John emerged with his arms full of four jars of

tomatoes. He put them on the ground.

"Wh-Wh-What are you going to do with those?" I queried suspiciously.

"Well, your grandmother and her gr-gr-grandmother and h-h-her grandmother before her all knew that the only thing that will kill the s-s-smell of skunk is tomatoes. S-Seems a shame to waste all these good tomatoes on a b-boy that can't l-l-look carefully at the w-w-world."

As he spoke, he unscrewed the zinc lids from the jars and poured the slimy vegetables over my head. It was one of the ugliest feelings I'd ever felt. The larger pieces slid slowly like garden slugs crawling down my back.

When the contents of all four jars had cascaded across my naked body, he picked up a sponge. Dipping it into the sauce at the bottom of the tub, he gave me a rough, thorough scrubbing.

He picked up the abalone shell and poured juice over my head. I felt like I was being re-baptized. As he massaged the bright red sauce into my hair, his face was covered by a sly grin.

"If the f-f-folks at the Baptist Church of P-P-Peter-the-Rock could see you now, they'd th-th-think for sure you were b-b-being washed in the b-blood of the L-L-Lamb."

"I d-d-don't know what that m-m-means."

"W-Well, it's an expression they're r-r-real f-fond of. It means that the b-b-blood of Jesus shed on the c-cross washes away folks' s-s-sins. N-N-Now I'll b-b-be the first to admit that you d-do smell sinful bad. B-B-But I think tomato j-j-juice works better than the b-b-blood of Jesus ever would when it comes to skunk smell."

He handed me a wooden washboard and instructed me on how to rub the tomato juice into my overalls. My Hermit Uncle John brought out a copper wash boiler and filled it at the pump. He took my overalls and rinsed them in the boiler.

As he wrung them out and prepared to hang them on the clothesline, he exclaimed, "Th-Th-There's something about these clothes of yours that still smells. D-D-Didn't you wash them good in the j-j-juice?"

I nodded. He felt in all the pockets and found nothing. He unsnapped the bib pocket. He took out my teddy bear. The gentle breeze carried the horrendous odor of skunk from the little creature. Encased in the bib's heavy fabric, it had escaped the scrubbing.

My Uncle John roared with laughter. He dropped the bear into the bottom of the tub. I squeezed the scarlet juice through my constant companion. I shuddered at the momentary vision of my bear hanging on the cross with blood flowing from his pierced side. The bear *had* saved me from a lot of grief, just like folk were always saying Jesus did.

Uncle John dumped the water from the boiler, pumped it full again and rinsed the bear. Then he hung my friend by its ear to dry in the hot morning sun alongside the overalls ballooning in the light wind.

He walked me down to the nearby lake. I rinsed myself off in the shallow water at the edge of the shore. Only the merest whiff of skunk odor clung to the area.

During the course of the morning, while clothes and bear dried, I helped my Hermit Uncle John prepare an expansion of his garden in which he could raise muskmelons. My worst fears were realized. He dug up some human bones. They were so small and delicate that they must have been part of an infant's skeleton.

Seeing my expression he said softly, "Don't b-b-be afraid. They're simply b-b-bare bones. Take them g-gently up to the rock point where we were last night. If you f-f-feel a special P-P-Presence, count yourself b-blessed. You'll be touched by the d-d-deepest springs of the sacred."

Naked, I carried the bare bones to the tip of the rock. I stood for a moment cradling the tiny relics from the past in my arms. Did I hear weeping around me? Was there a tug at the bones which had once encased a beating heart?

I knelt at the tip of the rock and laid the skeletal parts down on a patch of soft grey lichen with the same gentleness one would use to lay a baby on a blanket. I felt awkward. It seemed like I should do or say something.

I searched for a song that might be appropriate. I began to croon "Rock-a-bye Baby." I alternated it with "Jesus Loves Me." The weeping from the invisible Presence faded.

After a long time, I rose. Though streaked with dust from the digging and the bones, I felt clean. Though haunted by my daddy's whip, I felt whole. Though often shattered by my grief and anger, I felt, for the moment, healed.

As I walked down from the rock, I whispered, "Good-bye, good friends. Thank you."

Dear Gletha,

A dumb thing happened to me. I forgot what you taught me about looking at the world real close. I got sprayed by a skunk I mistook for Uncle John's pet skunk. I had to have tomatoes dumped over me.

I wonder when I'm going to learn to move slower through the world. You were always trying to get me to do that.

I miss you a lot.

Love,

Roger

P. S. I hope you noticed that I didn't get mad on paper over the fact that you called me "Rogee" in writing.

Dear Rogee,

I'm glad I wasn't there when the skunk got you. I won't even say "I warned you" about disturbing the quiet at the heart of the world and running roughshod over things.

I've always hoped that you'd stop long enough to feel things—even your pain from your daddy. You need to feel the hurtful things and then let them go. Sometimes I think you're just letting them stack up inside and then you try to outrun them.

I wish I could send you a loon's song.

Love,

Gletha

A LESSON IN SELF-DEFENSE

It was late August. The oats and the barley looked beautiful that year. My daddy's darknesses were farther apart when the future seemed a bit more hopeful. I'd gone a full three weeks without a beating.

Dad and I sat at sundown beneath the great elms at the field's edge. "Kid," he said, "smell that ripenin' grain."

I drew a deep breath. The sun-warmed barley smelled like the air which swirled out of the Dew Drop Inn in Pheasant Valley on a warm Saturday night.

He continued, "Tomorrow I start the harvest. I want you to head over to Lake Sumach early in the morning and see if you can git that dumb brother of mine to come out of hiding long enough to shock a little grain."

I flared, "Don't you ever call him d-d-dumb! He's one of the smartest men in the whole world. He spends a lot of time r-r-readin' his beautiful books. N-N-No way is he dumb."

Dad looked at me strangely, his face shadowed with pain. "You really do favor him over me, don't yuh, kid? Why the hell don't you just go and live with him? You spend so much time there, you might as well."

I thought for a moment that he was going to plunge immediately into one of his horrendous depressions. I shoved my frail hand into his large, calloused fist. "I d-d-don't really favor him," I lied. "I jist like to go f-f-fishing with him—and I really like his stories. I'll tell you what: I'm big enough this year to sp-sp-spend all d-day and half the night following the b-b-binder. I can pick up the grain sheaves and stand them in shocks. You jist wait and see if I c-c-can't work as hard as any m-m-man."

The prospect pleased him. He squeezed my hand and grinned one of the only grins I ever remember breaking up the permanent frown on his face.

Twilight deepened. The western sky looked like the lake of fire threatened by evangelists who set up their tents in town in the open lot by the gas station with the sign of the Flying Red Horse. In my mind's eye I could see the struggles of the lost souls reflected in the dying light. I shuddered.

My father, touched by the moment's mystery, stiffened. "What do you suppose that is comin' this way?"

My eye followed his pointing finger. The last blood-red ray of the setting sun illumined a stark white figure. It seemed to be floating slowly out of the west toward our farm.

I knew immediately what it was. It was the ghost of Gus McClittherd whose farm was next to ours. Gus had fathered thirteen children on his wife Em. One day Dad and he were talking over the line fence. They talked for a long time. I got bored and sat on the ground nearby making dandelion chains. When I tuned back into the conversation, it was to hear Gus comment mournfully, "Frank, she just ain't interested in it anymore."

Thunder began to rumble in the distance. The conversation broke off so everybody could get home before the rain hit. I wasn't sure what "it" was that Em was no longer interested in, but it must have been pretty important because later on that evening as we were feasting on fried fresh butchered pork liver Dad said something to Mom about if Em didn't mend her ways Gus'd start looking for "it" somewhere else. The thunder crashed dramatically outside. With a glance at me my mother put her finger to her lips and shushed my father's narrative to a halt. I thought it would be right neighborly to help Gus find whatever it was he'd lost. However, something in the air warned me that silence was the better part of valor.

Some weeks later the whole of Sunrise Township was shocked to hear that Gus had been shot by Raymie Collins in the Collins' house in Pheasant Valley. Raymie was a railroad man. He was often away for days at a time. He'd returned unexpectedly and found Gus looking for "it" in bed with Raymie's wife Hazel right out in broad daylight. He'd taken his target pistol and plugged Gus. The neighbors had come running. Some of them carried the dying Gus to the little hospital where old Doc Workington did his level best to save him. Gus's lungs filled with blood too fast.

Gracie Grundstrap who lived next door jumped in her rattletrap Chevy and headed to the country to fetch Em. Em arrived at Gus's bedside just before the end. Gus's final words were widely reported by Gracie who'd kept her arms around Em as she knelt at her husband's bedside. Gus was purported to have said, "Woman, if I die, I'll come back and haunt you for driving me to my death with your coldness."

It was probably just as well that Gus's lungs finished filling and he was incapable of further utterances before he died.

Now here in the dying rays of an August night was verification of Gracie's tale. An intense white figure was slowly moving over the fields toward the McClittherd farm. The moaning wind in the elms seemed to be bearing the ghastly visitor closer. My father whispered, "Don't move, kid. I'm going to grab my rifle. We don't want to be surprised by an unwelcome visitor."

I hardly needed to be told not to move. I was absolutely rigid. I doubted the wisdom of my father's action. Gus had already been shot once. I didn't think a second bullet would halt the impending specter.

Dad appeared silently at my side, rifle in readiness. The ghost changed its direction slightly and headed directly for us. I understood Gus's movement. He and Dad often hunted ducks together. They were forever bickering over who was the better shot. It would be just like Gus to fling a final taunt at my father from beyond the grave on his way to do in Em.

It was then that a strange sound assailed our ears. The foreign visitor was whistling! A crystal clear rendition of "Santa Lucia" floated over the fragrant, ripening fields. Miss Winkleman, the school music teacher, had taught the song to us. Since I couldn't carry a tune, I had to sit in a chair in the front of the classroom and pretend to be a gondolier in Venice rowing in rhythm to the song. The other children in the classroom wanted to sing it double-time just to see me sweat.

My father chuckled in relief. "That ain't the ghost of Gus McClittherd. He could never carry a tune in a gunnysack. Besides, I kind'a doubt that it's a ghost even. There seems to be a pair of legs extending below the white now that it's closer. Whatever or whoever it is is walkin' instead of floatin'."

The approaching figure took a running leap over the fence across the road and dropped into the ditch as if wanting to avoid being seen in the headlights of a car approaching slowly from the south.

After a few moments the figure reappeared and turned into our driveway. Brutus, the old gander in the chickenyard, honked loudly to herald the intrusion.

The figure spotted us and headed in our direction. Still uncertain as to the nature of the approaching being, I huddled close to my Dad. I felt his fingers tighten on the rifle. The countryside was alive with tales of marauding drifters in this Depression time of scarce money and few jobs.

Our fear was mitigated somewhat by the renewed outpouring of sound. I recognized some of the tunes as parts from Metropolitan Opera radio broadcasts I occasionally listened to surreptitiously on Saturday afternoons. If I was caught, my father's belt went into action for wasting the radio batteries on that "highfalutin' stuff." Battery power was to be reserved for "Ma Perkins," "Stella Dallas," Charles E. Fuller's "Old Fashioned Revival Hour" and "The Grand Ol' Opry." The latter was the only really legitimate opera in my parents' cultural lexicon.

The last light revealed a tall young man who moved toward us with lynx-like grace. He was just over six feet tall. The most memorable feature was his incredibly white shirt. Dad had picked up a flashlight along with the gun. He aimed the beam at the man's face. His dark skin set off teeth which matched his shirt and outlined a broad grin. Matted black curls framed a broad forehead.

He swept past us without a word. He merely doffed his white cloth cap as he went by. He headed toward the smallest of the fields. Dad had cut the barley there yesterday as a test run for getting the machinery in order. Bundles of grain were scattered ready to be shocked.

The white-shirted man began grabbing the bundles and placing them upright in perfect shocks. They were tilted in such a way that they would dry quickly if rain should fall.

Dad laid his gun on the bed of a nearby wagon. He watched the strange figure intently and commented, "I'll bet he'll last about fifteen minutes. Then he'll come crawling out of the field, expecting a full meal."

We sat watching the incredible performance for nearly an hour. Mom, missing us in the house, came out and joined the audience in the cool of the evening. They agreed that they hadn't ever seen such good work.

Having finished the little field, the figure floated and sang its way back toward us. Coming up even with our admiring trio, he again doffed his cap to my father, bowed to my mother and threw a piece of hard candy to me.

As he strode wordlessly down the driveway toward the gravel road, my father called after him, "Where do you think you're goin'? Git yerself right back here and answer a couple of questions."

The man broke his stride and turned back abruptly. In the process he kicked up a cloud of dust which smoked white in the moonlight, making him look for all the world like an illustration from Dante's *Inferno*.

He paused in front of my father who exploded, "What was that all about? You pass us by without a word, shock a field of our grain without any contract and then walk away without an 'if,' 'and' or 'but.' I think you've got some explainin' to do."

The stranger stepped forward and tousled my hair as he passed. He said, "Harvest is beginning. The workers are many. The jobs are few. I wanted to be better than anybody else. I stopped by for a little practice. I hope I didn't do anything wrong."

Dad replied, "There's somethin' fishy here. Nobody goes out an' does field work for nothin'.."

"Did I do it wrong or hurt anybody in the process? No? Well, then, I'll be on my way."

My mother caught the sleeve of his snow white shirt, saying, "You must be tired. At least pause long enough to have a little 'lunch.' After all, you shocked the barley for us. It'll only take a few minutes. By the way, what's your name? If you're going to be at our table, we should know your name."

"You've convinced me," he said. "I'll stay for a bit—if that's okay with your husband—oh, yes, and with your son as well. My name is Vincente Fuccio. You can call me Tey."

I liked him already. He'd included me in the decision as to whether or not he should stay.

My father said grudgingly, "I 'spose you should have a bite to eat. By the way, this is my wife Mary and my son Roger. Now, where are you headin'?"

As Tey answered, Mom headed across the darkening yard toward the kitchen. "Back to where I left my gear last night: in a straw stack three ditches to the south of here. I just came from town where I was...lookin' for work."

His hesitation caused a question to raise itself on my father's face. "You don't look drunk. You a drinker?"

Tey replied, "I'm a worker."

"Are you anything else?"

After a moment's hesitation Tey responded, "Not that I

know of."

"Well, all right. Boy, Vincente can wash up on the stand outside the kitchen door. Show him where it is."

We started across the yard toward the house. He smiled in the gathering dusk, put a hand on my shoulder and softly whistled "Santa Lucia."

I asked him if he'd please whistle something else. "Santa Lucia" made my arms hurt. I told him about my command performance at school.

He paused, knelt down and massaged my shoulders briskly. His touch felt good. He said, "Every time you hear the melody, remember the touch. The pain will go away."

He was right.

Mom had hung a lantern on the elm tree which shaded the kitchen at the height of summer. On a broad board suspended between two wooden apple boxes she'd placed the necessities for our unexpected guest: a washpan of warm water from the reservoir on the stove, a bar of homemade soap, a faded Turkish towel and the drinking bucket with its communal enameled cup. He carefully removed his gleaming shirt and hung it on a low branch. As he stepped into the arc of light, I saw it: a black-and-blue bruise on his temple. I'd experienced such bruises on my own body and seen them on my mother's arms after my father's beatings.

As he stood soaking his hands in the warm water, I blurted, "Tey, d-d-does your d-d-daddy beat you too?"

I bit my lip hard. The comment had slipped out. I was never to say nothing to nobody about my father's beatings as he slipped into his darknesses.

As I tasted the blood from my lacerated lip, Vincente looked at me strangely. He responded, "Yeah, my daddy beat me—but I haven't seen him in years. I guess all daddies beat their kids."

He lifted his hands from the water. On the back of his right hand was tattooed the most perfect rose I'd ever seen. His knuckles were badly skinned. He saw me staring.

"Oh, this. I had a little contest with a railroad guy in town earlier today. He lost—but not before he got in a couple of good punches. Say, kid, do you know how to fight?"

As a skinny stammerer with buck teeth I was the butt of playground derision. I dreamed of the day when I might miraculously retaliate with effective avenging fury.

"P-P-Please, can you teach me? I'd l-l-like to kill the Gunderson boys. They're always t-t-teasing me."

"Well, if your Pa takes me on to work during harvest, I'll see if I can't make you the lightweight champeen of this little corner of the entire universe."

As he soaped his armpits and chest, I looked up at the Milky Way glowing above us and felt a little more hopeful about my corner of the universe.

He dumped the water from the washpan on some nearby zinnias. He refilled the pan with cold water from the bucket. Bending over, he poured the water over his torso and head. He sputtered and wheezed like a horse on a winter morning.

As he straightened up and disappeared into the depths of the great soft towel, something fell to the ground. I quickly bent and picked up the object. I turned so that the light from the lantern fell fully upon an embossed leather sheath. Intricate flowers and leaves flowed to its slender point. From the sheath extended a short silver handle. A mermaid with a death's head in her navel glowed in the dull light.

Mesmerized, I slowly drew the object from its tight case. The sea creature was balanced on the thinnest, narrowest blade I'd ever seen.

Suddenly, my wrist was encircled in a tight grip. Tey's voice hissed in my ear.

"Careful, boy. I don't want you to hurt yourself with my haunted blade."

He gently removed the knife and its sheath from my hands. Reaching for his shirt, he stepped out of the light to the other side of the elm's wide trunk. He returned in a moment. The knife was nowhere to be seen.

He knelt on one knee in front of me. He put his hands on my shoulders and drew me close. Looking me straight in the eyes he said, "That knife is called a stiletto. It's the only thing I have from my daddy. The story has it that it's been in our family for over five hundred years. There's a lot of silly talk about how it's haunted—how the ghosts of all the folk it's killed hover 'round it and drive whoever has it to kill again. There are those who would like to get their hands on it. I'd appreciate your not talking about it to nobody. A loose tongue could get me into a heap of trouble."

His voice held a hard-edged threatening note that scared me. I was silent for a moment. Then I ran out *my* request: "I w-w-won't say n-n-nothing about the stiletto if you w-w-won't say n-n-nothing about my daddy beating mom and me. I'm not supposed to tell."

His face softened. He drew me into a tight embrace and said, "That feels good, Rog. We'll protect each other's secrets—forever."

My mother appeared at the back door. "Tey, you come and eat this food while it's hot. Don't let that boy keep you out here with his foolishness."

I followed him into the kitchen. Spread out on the table was one of my mother's famous "little lunches" served at any hour of the day or night when folks happened by. There was a plate heaped up with fried liver, leftover mashed potatoes drenched in butter, fresh sliced tomatoes and homemade bread. The plate was circled with side dishes of applesauce, canned peaches and lime Jello with marshmallows. The feast was completed by a cut-glass pitcher of grape Kool-Aid.

Tey appeared overwhelmed by her largess. However, to my mother's delight he consumed everything in sight. Sitting at his side in silent wonder, I nibbled molasses cookies from the platter that graced the table center as the victuals disappeared. Not a word was spoken. Mother hovered just in case our guest could possibly desire more.

She heard my father approaching from the barn. She

rushed out with a teakettle full of warm water. I heard it sloshing in the metal washpan as he cleaned up outside the door.

He came in, surveyed the empty dishes Mom was even now clearing away, and sat down at the table. A cup of coffee appeared automatically at his elbow. He reached for a handful of cookies.

"Well, I feel better about the little uninvited job you did out in the field now that you've filled your belly. I don't know nothin' about you, but if that's any indication, you're a good worker. I could use some help for a couple of weeks. I can't pay you much. But you can sleep in the barn and the eats are good."

Tey smiled. "I think this will be a fine break. I want to end up in California one of these days. I'll walk across the fields tonight to where I left my bag in a straw stack. I'll probably sleep there. I'll see you in the morning."

I pleaded, "C-C-Can I walk a little ways with you, Tey?"

"Whoa!" interrupted my father. "I think a boy should respect his elders. He should call you Mr. Fuccio—or at least Vincente."

Tey responded, "Every kid needs one adult who they can call something special. I like your boy. I've given him, and anyone else in the family, permission to call me Tey. Rog, you can walk with me as far as the road, if it's okay with your folks."

They nodded silent assent.

We stepped outside. He put an arm around my shoulders. To be touched gently felt good. Reaching the mailbox by the roadside, Tey squatted down and said, "Remember our secrets."

He strode off toward the south following the fence rows. He began belting out "Celeste di Aida." The planet Venus, hanging low on the horizon, seemed to twinkle more intensely with the rising notes.

The following morning when the folks got up at 5:30, two

pails of milk were sitting on the washstand outside the kitchen door. In a distant field, sheaves of grain were being quickly shocked by a lone figure.

Dad fed the livestock while Mom got breakfast. I was sent to fetch Tey. He said he couldn't sleep so he'd moved over in the middle of the night. At sunup, he decided he might as well do something and proceeded to do it.

As we walked across the fields glowing in the intense light of the rising sun, Tey commented thoughtfully, "If I'm gonna' make a topnotch fighter out of you, I'd better begin right away."

I clenched my hands into tight fists and began dancing around him as I'd seen the tough sixth-graders do in the schoolyard. He laughed and shook his head saying, "That's not quite lesson one. Your form is terrible."

The flat topped tip of a granite boulder reared itself five feet above the ground on the fence line we were passing. Tey grabbed me, swung me up and stood me on the rock.

Stepping back, he said, "Jump to me, boy."

Expecting him to catch me, I leaped fearlessly toward him. He stepped back, and I plummeted to the sun-baked earth. My breath was jolted out of me.

My dad had impressed upon me the fact that I could never do anything right. The fact that I was shuddering in pain on the ground surely must have been my fault. As I looked up at Tey, the prisms of my tears enlarged his eyes, and I encountered a great, uncaring, staring mask. I blinked and he was Tey again.

He picked me up and stood me on the rock a second time. He stepped back and said, "We'd better try that again."

This time I was determined to do it right. I crouched and, aiming myself directly at him, I leapt from my perch.

He quickly sidestepped. Again, I hit the earth, barking my knee on a sharp stone through a hole in my overalls. I felt totally betrayed as I lay sobbing face down in the dirt.

He lifted me roughly from the ground and stood me on the rock once more. Two crows circled above, cawing harshly. In a voice as violent as my father's at his worst Tey shouted at me, "Jump to me, boy!"

I was dizzy with fear. My legs gave way. I toppled from the heights into the soft grass which grew in the shadow of the rock. I tried to squiggle under the boulder's protecting edge.

Then I felt his hands gently prying me out from the granite overhang. He held me in his arms for a long time as I sobbed out my confusion. He whispered, "You've just learned the first lesson of self-defense. *Never trust anybody.*"

My arms circled him tightly. I felt loved and safe once more until my fingers encountered the solid object extending above his belt under the back of his shirt. My finger traced the outline of the mermaid with the death's head in her navel.

Dear Gletha,

I'm scared to death. I have just made a new friend who is teaching me how to fight so I don't have to be such a sissy anymore and he's sort of the big brother I've always wanted but he carries the most beautiful knife in the world and I'm worried and I know I should put some periods in this sentence the way you taught me but I'm too scared to stop long enough to do that.

His knife has a death's head on it. But it's almost as if I can see death at his shoulder. Write to me right away. This all may not make sense but it's pretty hard to make sense when you're scared.

Love,

Roger

Dear Rogee,

Remember when you went off to school that morning and Dilly Fenn was going to fight you? I said I'd be with you in a special way so you wouldn't have to be afraid.

Remember that now. Love knows no geography and I love you.

Something else. You may not understand this right away, but you've got the rest of your life to think about it. Death is always at your shoulder. You've just got to find ways to make death your friend.

Love,

Gletha

LOVE, VINCENTE

The early morning sunlight streaming through the kitchen window focused on the platter of bacon and eggs in the center of the breakfast table presided over by my father. The soft yolks glistened like smaller suns. Mom was adding dry corncobs to the cookstove so that the lids would be the proper temperature to toast bread.

Tey and I slipped into our places. Dad handed him the platter.

The air was filled with the smell of crisping bread. The harsh scrape of the turner caterpillared the hair on the back of my neck as Mom flipped the thick golden slices soon to be spread with home-churned butter (my shoulders ached at the memory) and chokecherry jelly.

Tey groaned with pleasure, pushed back from the table and said, "I'd better waddle to the field while I can still move. You may have to cover me with barley bundles and leave me there until I can sleep off my breakfast."

My father turned to me: "You head for the lake and roust out my useless brother. Even with this Italian cyclone at work I could use some extra help."

I started to make a comeback at him, but my mother stared the words back into me with a hard look.

I wended my way through meadowlark song and pheasant

calls. Wisps of morning fog—or was it smoke?—lifted from the tip of the great granite outcropping.

My Hermit Uncle John was sitting with his back to the door so he could look through the window at the early morning sunlight glinting off the lake. The ever present *Holy Bible* was open in his hand. Pity Me, his pet skunk, was asleep at his feet. A dreaming Tiny unconsciously growled from his lap. He was reading aloud. I listened to the sacred words which he read without a stammer.

> Judge me, O Lord; for I have walked in mine integrity: I have trusted also in the Lord; therefore I shall not slide.
>
> Examine me, O Lord, and prove me; try my reins and my heart.
>
> For thy loving kindness is before mine eyes and I have walked in thy truth.
>
> I have not sat with vain persons, neither will I go in with dissemblers.
>
> I have hated the congregation of evildoers; and will not sit with the wicked.
>
> I will wash mine hands in innocence: so will I compass thy altar, O Lord, that I may publish with the voice of thanksgiving and tell of all thy wondrous works.
>
> Lord, I have loved the habitation of thy house, and the place where thine honor dwelleth.
>
> Gather not my soul with sinners, nor my life with bloody men in whose hands is mischief and their right hand is full of bribes.
>
> But as for me, I will walk in mine integrity. Redeem me and be merciful unto me.
>
> My foot standeth in an even place. In the congregations will I bless the Lord.

As he read, his voice became more choked. He turned his

head when I entered. I saw he'd been crying.

I put my hand on his shoulder. "Wh-Wh-What's the m-m-matter, Uncle John?"

"I went to the store last night. Gr-Gr-Greg Gr-Gr-Griggs had just come out from town. They found B-Barney Beenockle dead behind the g-g-grain elevator."

"What did he d-d-die from?" I asked.

"The coroner couldn't r-r-really find out. Somebody'd said he'd been in a fight with a drifter. Then he'd disappeared till the patrol car found him in the mud. S-S-Seems his left lung had collapsed. His knuckles were skinned bad.

"I f-f-feel real sorrowful about him. He was a little qu-qu-queer in his head, but 'ceptin' when he was drunk, he was real gentle. When I first m-m-moved out here, he and some of the guys from town used to get drunk up there on Shaman's Point. Then B-B-Barney would strip and j-j-jump into the deep water below. When he came walkin' out of the l-l-lake, he looked like a great b-b-brown bear 'cause he was covered all over w-with the longest hair you could ever imagine on a human body.

"When I d-discovered my other friends hovering around the r-r-rock, I asked the guys not to c-come back and frighten them off maybe. Barney made sure they never gave me no trouble."

"Wh-Wh-Why would anyone ever want to kill Barney?" I queried.

"H-H-He could be r-r-real mean when he was drunk. He w-w-was always sayin' he was going to k-kill somebody. He d-d-didn't know his own strength."

I felt a strange sinking inside me accompanied by visions of the death's head in the mermaid's navel and the incredibly narrow stiletto blade.

My reverie was broken by Uncle John asking, "You s-s-seem to be in pretty g-good shape for somebody who usually c-c-comes to see me only after he's been beaten."

"Dad wanted some help with the shocking so he sent me to f-f-fetch you. Then a guy lookin' for work came by, and he's real good, but Dad still wanted you. If y-y-you don't come, he's liable to beat me."

John's face clouded. "I haven't s-s-seen him for months since I ran into him fishing across the lake. He d-d-didn't even speak to me then. I don't know why folks g-gotta' hurt folks with their tongues and fists and s-s-silence. I don't mind helpin' out, b-but I wish there wasn't so much pain in the air whenever we're t-t-together.

"But it will probably do me good to w-w-work away from here. I might not think so much about B-B-Barney."

As we walked across the fields, I told him about Vincente. For the first time since we'd met I didn't *quite* tell him everything. Knowing how he felt about fighting, I spared him the details of our first lesson.

Since Tey and I had made a mutual promise, I also didn't share with him our secret.

By the time we'd reached our fields, the sun had dried the dew. My father had the horses hitched to the binder and was littering the stubble with bundles of grain.

I introduced my Hermit Uncle John to Tey, trying as I did to give "Vincente Fuccio" its proper operatic lilt. Uncle John took his hand, looked at him deeply, nodded curtly and turned to pick up the nearest bundle, leaning it against its neighbor.

Tey blushed and moved in the opposite direction.

As the day progressed, the field was teepeed with shocks. Communication was sparse. Uncle John tried to greet my father warmly. What old enmity there was remained in place. When Tey tried to speak with Uncle John, he got stammered, brief phrases in response.

I tried to chatter to whichever one was near me. Each adult was lost in his own inner world.

Three weeks passed. The harvest was nearly over. Uncle John did not return after that first day. He finished a piece of Mom's apple pie and disappeared into the moonlight. My father never mentioned his abrupt exit.

Tey continued his whirlwind work patterns. When there

was nothing to do in the fields, Dad put him to creosoting fenceposts. It was hot, smelly work, smearing the wood with the acrid black substance to keep it from rotting. Tey never complained.

There were times when he'd disappear for a few hours and return smelling of beer. His step never wavered. Perhaps he would belt out "Santa Lucia" a bit more loudly.

Tey spent every non-working moment with me. We had our special place out in the walnut grove where he would teach me to box. One day, my hand shot out with surprising expertise and caught him unexpectedly on the nose. Blood immediately poured from his nostrils.

I burst into tears. Pulling a soiled bandana from my pocket, I pressed it to his face. He was laughing.

"You've finally made it, Rog. You're a real fighter. You've drawn your first blood. Now you're ready to take revenge."

"What's r-r-revenge?" I asked.

He paused for a long moment and looked deep into my eyes. "If anyone ever hurts or wrongs a person you love, make 'em pay for it in spades. Don't ever give up until you find 'em and MAKE...'EM...PAY. You're old enough to draw blood. You're old enough to be a real man and take revenge."

He knelt in front of me. His eyes reflected the dark clouds of the summer storm gathering in the east. He grabbed my wrist in his left hand and held up my arm. A fresh scratch from a gooseberry bush thorn marred the soft white underside. Lifting his right hand, Tey smeared blood from his nostril on his index finger and touched it to my wound.

"We're really brothers now. Our blood's been mingled. I'll always care for you. Will you swear to care for me?"

I grabbed him around the neck and held my cheek against his, ignoring the scratching of a two-day stubble.

I sobbed, "I'll always c-c-care for you, Tey. I'll never, never forget you. Wherever you are, I'll c-c-come to you if you n-need me."

He started to cry. Tears on our touching cheeks mingled as had our blood on my arm.

The moment was shattered by the discordant cry of a crow in the top of the sheltering walnut tree and the low rumble of thunder from the approaching storm.

He made us wooden swords, and we pretended to be knights fighting for a fair lady's hand. He carved daggers, and we slashed at each other with great abandon. Always, the games were violent.

The moments of violence were tempered by moments of tenderness. We'd walk down the country roads, his hand on my shoulder. I sometimes fantasized that he was the brother I never had.

During those weeks I did not visit my Hermit Uncle John. As long as Tey was sleeping in the barn and helping with the chores, my father seemed to elude his darknesses, and I remained unscathed. Fascinated by the new, I neglected the healing old.

Late one night Tey came singing across the fields. His voice had a harshly strident edge. My parents looked knowingly at one another in the lamplight.

My father commented sadly, "I think he's drinking more. He's done about everything I need. He'd better be on his way to California."

I panicked. I did not want to lose my brother-friend. I slipped outside without slamming the screen door and rushed toward the song.

As I approached, he grabbed me and threw me in the air as he always did. He caught me. In that instant the harsh moonlight illumined his battered face. I smelled whiskey on his breath.

I slid down his body as if it were a fireman's pole. As I hit the ground, my fingers sought out the characteristic bulge at the back of his pants. It was not there.

"T-T-Tey, it's gone! Your stiletto. It's gone!"

His hand shot around and probed his belt line. He

exploded: "Omigod! I've got to find it."

Shoving me brusquely away, he turned and ran across the fields toward Pheasant Valley.

He didn't return that night. Nor the next day. Nor the next.

I slipped up to the corner of the haymow where he slept. In a neat bundle were two intensely white shirts which my mother had washed for him and hung out in the bright August sun. There was a pair of dark trousers, some underwear and socks, shaving things and an envelope.

I felt a bit guilty as I opened his private belongings. But it was okay. After all, we were blood brothers.

The envelope contained a folded piece of paper and two photos. I removed the paper first. To my amazement it was written to me:

Rog,

If you should ever have cause to look through my things, it will probably be because I've disappeared. I just wanted you to know that you are the best thing that has happened in my life in a long time. Remember everything I've taught you. It's the only way to survive in this dirty world. The pictures will explain to you what I'm trying to find—the one who killed the only woman I've ever cared about. You're the second person I've really cared about.

Love,

Vincente

Removing the photos, I stared into the eyes of a dark-haired young woman. Across the back was scrawled a single word: "Rosa."

The second was a close-up of the same woman. She seemed to be asleep. Resting against her cheek was a hand tattooed with a perfect rose. The thumb and forefinger lightly held the blade of a stiletto. Extending across the back of the hovering hand was the handle. It was carved in the shape of a mermaid with a death's head in her navel.

It took me a long moment to realize that the picture was outlined in ruffled white satin. I'd seen pictures of dead relatives in their coffins. I realized it was a picture of the young woman in hers.

The picture was punctured in places by something written on the back. Turning it over, angry letters met my eye, spelling out ROSA—REVENGE. A cold chill shook me.

I almost fell down the ladder from the haymow. I ran full-tilt across the fields toward the protection of the forest and the cabin of my Hermit Uncle John.

The setting sun, burning blood-red into the west, dipped itself halfway into the holy lake. The bloated moon, half risen in the east, seemed to balance the sky.

I rushed into his cabin. He was seated in the living room reading *The Decline and Fall of the Roman Empire*. I paused in the doorway. Tears were streaming down his cheeks. As he watched the vanishing light, I heard him whisper, "So many deaths. So many deaths."

He turned and saw me standing there. He brightened: "R-R-Rog. It's been a long time s-s-since you've b-b-been here. C-C-Come over here and let me h-h-hug you."

He put the book on the shelf and gathered me into his arms. I started to sob. As he held me, I choked out everything I knew about Vincente.

He embraced me for a long time until my sobs subsided. Then he said quietly, "Let's w-w-wander across the fields to Pheasant Valley. We'll k-k-keep our eyes and ears open and s-s-see what we can find out. There's bound to b-b-be gossip around t-t-town."

And then, to make me laugh, he commented further, "You never know. At least we m-m-might find one of T-Tillie Ingebretsen's sh-sh-sheets!"

A freak cyclone had wailed through the countryside two weeks earlier. The only recorded damage was to Old Maid

Tillie's house. It had been picked up with its inhabitant and whirled a mile through the air. When the created vacuum caused the shack to collapse, Tillie was dropped into Garrett Maguire's shallow farm pond where he mistook her for a bundle of rags until he heard her lamenting, "They're gone! My sheets. My beautiful sheets! I'll never see them again."

Garrett waded in and carried her out of the water, discovering in the process that she had survived without a scratch. Later he would find one of her tortoise-shell combs driven by the storm's incredible power into a fence post on the pond's edge.

Her only sorrow was the loss of her pride and joy: her sheets which were the whitest in the township. She'd won a blue ribbon at the county fair for the delicacy of their embroidered borders of mourning doves and violets. Cynics commented that the doves were in mourning over the unmarried state of their creator.

Every preacher in the county invited Tillie to witness in his church to the saving grace of God evident in her unscathed life. The Baptists across the lake at Peter-the-Rock were particularly charmed by her tale. Tillie took each occasion to plead for the return of her prize sheets.

The farmers who gathered for early morning coffee at the Dew Drop Inn speculated that anybody who returned one of Tillie's sheets could have Tillie for the asking. There was great hilarity when Rorick Hegerson, a bachelor, found one wrapped around his windmill tower. He shamefacedly gave it to Garrett's wife, Madge, to return, saying, "I just don't want to take a chance."

When Uncle John raised the question, I said, "I h-h-hope we f-f-find one. Iffen she'd m-m-marry you, you wouldn't have t-t-to live alone."

He responded quietly, "N-N-Nobody, not even Tillie Ingebretsen would w-want me as I am. Besides, I've g-g-got Pity Me, Tiny and you."

We hiked across the fields lighted by the dying sun and

rising moon. Every ditch and low spot was filled with water from the storm which had accompanied the freak wind that whirled Tillie into fame.

Near Pheasant Valley we walked down a lane that led from Gabby Tilson's place. It crossed the South Central railroad tracks. A few yards from the crossing a patch of white shown in the uncertain light.

"L-L-Look, Uncle John. It's one of Tillie's sheets. I'll get it for you."

"D-D-Don't bother. Just l-l-leave well enough alone."

I didn't listen. I scrambled quickly down the embankment. I discovered that it was indeed a sheet. I picked it up and was momentarily surprised to find that its edges had been weighted with stones.

As I lifted the expanse of whiteness, a scream tore itself from my heart. Spread-eagled beneath the sheet was the lifeless body of Vincente.

At the sound of my cry Uncle John slid down the bank to my side. He grabbed me and stood there speechless. Our eyes began to take in details of the scene. He'd lain three days in the hot August sun. Maggots had begun their work.

Then I saw it. Extending from the upper left side of his back was the graceful mermaid with the death's head in her navel. Bluebottle flies clustered around the entry point. I knelt down quickly. As if life might return to his body as the result of my action, I withdrew the stiletto. The flies did not move.

I wiped the weapon carefully on the edge of the sheet. I mingled Tey's blood with the fine embroidery. The mourning doves now had a reason for their sadness. I unsnapped the wide pocket of my bib overalls. I nestled the stiletto against the ever present teddy bear.

Uncle John, sobbing as he held me, said sharply, "G-G-Give me the knife, Rog."

"N-N-No. Tey and I were blood br-br-brothers. He taught me to fight real g-good. Someday I'll find who d-d-done this. He'll not live long."

Uncle John grabbed me by the shoulders and knelt down to eye level with me. "Boy, there's b-b-been enough violence already. I was in the store t-t-two nights ago. I heard f-folks talkin' about bad blood between two drunken D-D-Dagos. One of them supposedly carried a h-h-haunted knife.

"T-T-Tino Milo has worked for the railroad f-for a long time. He appeared out of nowhere a f-f-few years ago.

"My g-guess is that T-T-Tey'd been hunting him. We probably kn-kn-know the reason. When Tey dropped his knife in a br-br-brawl with T-T-Tino, Tino f-f-found it. When Tey w-w-went back to get the stiletto, Tino killed him. Tino brought him out here on a railroad h-handcar, dumped the body over the embankment and f-f-for some r-reason or other c-c-covered him with one of T-T-Tillie's sheets which the cyclone bl-bl-blowed into the d-d-ditch.

"N-N-Now, boy, give me the knife like I told you."

I responded, "I can't, Uncle John. I-I-I promised Tey I'd get r-r-revenge on whoever hurt him. I p-probably should wait till I'm a l-l-little bigger. But Tey said I w-w-was a real good fighter right now. I've already drawn blood."

With a lightning move of his hand Uncle John grabbed the front of my overalls, unsnapped the pocket and removed the weapon. He pulled out his shirttail in the back, slipped the stiletto beneath his belt and tucked in his shirt once more.

He ordered me, "You s-s-sit here with your f-friend. I'll g-g-go into town and fetch the sheriff. Wh-Wh-When he arrives, let's not say anything about the h-h-haunted knife."

I begged him, "D-Do me a favor. They musta' taught you to k-k-kill real good when they were g-g-getting you ready to be a soldier. F-Find that stinkin' Tino Milo and s-s-slip the blade between his r-r-ribs. You're p-part of my family. Since T-T-Tey and I were blood brothers, you c-c-can take revenge as well as me."

Tears welled up once more in the dying light. Uncle John said quietly, "L-L-Listen to me, Rog. I got this way from lookin' at too much death. When I was escapin' f-from the

Battle of the Marne, I st-st-stumbled over young German bodies and young F-F-French b-bodies and young American b-b-bodies, some of whom I grew up with. We w-w-were dyin' in a war of revenge wh-wh-which captured the whole world. There's another war goin' on now. All that will c-c-come of it is more d-d-dead young bodies. There won't n-never be no peace till r-r-revenge is stopped."

He turned and walked away in the moonlight toward Pheasant Valley.

The temperature dropped quickly. I pulled Tillie's sheet over Tey as if to warm him once more. Ground fog ghosted around us.

A half-hour passed. In the distance I heard a railroad handcar approaching. Was Tino Milo revisiting the scene of the disposal of his crime? I was frozen in fear.

Then I heard Uncle John's voice calling, "R-R-Rog, it's okay. We're almost t-t-to you."

I warmed with relief. Four figures stepped off the little carrier. Uncle John had found the sheriff, Mel Merkin, in the Dew Drop Inn. Pulling them quickly from their beers, Mel had deputized Rorick Hegerson and Garrett Maguire.

I told them everything I knew. After a cursory examination by flashlight of the corpse and the area, the sheriff told Rorick to stand guard for the night. He didn't want the body moved until morning for fear of destroying evidence, though he suspected who the murderer was. He hoped the murder weapon could be found.

Rorick Hegerson was doomed to spend the night not only in the presence of a corpse but in the presence of Tillie Ingebretsen's sheet.

Uncle John began moving across the fields. I turned without another look at the body of my friend outlined beneath the fog-dampened sheet.

I called to him, "Good n-n-night, Uncle John. I think I'll head f-for home."

He turned and said, "I think w-w-we've got one more thing

to d-d-do if we're g-going to st-st-st-stop the endless circle of v-violence."

I followed him. We took every shortcut possible as we headed for his homestead. Tiny dashed out to greet us, sniffing our pantlegs to check us out for having been in the environs of any other dogs.

We did not stop at the shack. Uncle John headed silently for the shore.

We walked out on a great flat rock beside which a crystal spring bubbled up and connected with the main body of water.

The wind rose sobbing in the trees. I heard another sound like crying in the distance. Did it come from the unseen throats of Uncle John's spirit friends?

I looked up at the tip of the great granite outcropping towering above us, now silhouetted against the full moon. A red fire glowed on its tip, giving the moon the same cast of blood which the sun had borne before it. The surrounding stars were painfully bright.

Uncle John was standing at the very lip of the lower rock. His shirttail was out, and I saw that he was holding the stiletto by the tip of its blade and extending it toward the heavens. A firefly alighted on the mermaid's navel and flickered there, extinguishing the image of death.

He drew back his arm and hurled the stiletto high into the starlight. It arced smoothly upwards, then plunged gracefully toward the dark water. The haunted weapon disappeared noiselessly beneath the surface of the holy lake.

He turned to stare at the granite point. He whispered, "Good night, my friends. May at least one circle of violence have been broken."

The red fire flamed brightly for a moment and then went out.

Dear Gletha,

I'm real sad tonight. The last time I wrote to you I was scared. You're right. I guess death is always at our shoulders. Vincente (he let me call him "Tey") was killed by his own knife. He'd become my blood brother in a special way. But he was awful angry inside. I guess you never know what you'll do when you're that angry inside.

I remember falling into the sunken grave and you coming and our seeing the little skull with the moccasin flower growing from the left eye socket. You told me there might be a special way that folk might live forever.

I hope Vincente does.

Love,

Roger

Dear Rogee,

I've been real busy. The weather's been right for gathering herbs. I miss you working along with me.

I wish I could send you a few leaves of something to boil up and drink and heal your sadness. Your friend was destroyed by the anger he picked up somewhere more than by his knife. I hope you can remember that your daddy's anger won't destroy you unless you let it. There'd be a lot fewer folk destroying themselves and others if they learned that.

I'm late with the milking and the goats are letting me know.

Love,

Gletha

THE SOLDIER BOY

Sherm Savola stood over my desk in Miss Maupin's fifth grade classroom. He looked at me appraisingly and then said, "Stand up, Rog. I want to see just how tall you are."

I was a little frightened. Mr. Savola was the high school band director. He came over to the grade school to give lessons. He was a big man with coal-black curly hair and a pencil-line black moustache. When he passed down the halls, you heard the cadence of invisible snare drums. He shimmered as he walked.

And now this splendid, admired man was speaking to *me*! I didn't think he even knew I was alive. I struggled out of my desk and stood uncertainly before him. He glanced at my gangly body which, due to a recent growth spurt, was pushing 5' 10" before the rest of my peers.

His rich bass voice stunned me with a question: "How would you like to march with the high school band? With a school as small as Pheasant Valley I need some fill-ins for the football season, and you're one of the only people around tall enough to do it. We're buying new uniforms, so you'll look good. I'll give you an instrument to carry. You can fake it. What do you say? We rehearse after school so you won't miss any classes. Your folks needn't worry about your getting home. Band members ride the team bus."

I was dumbfounded. I didn't know *what* to say. I finally stammered out, "I-I-I think I'd like that. B-B-But m-m-my daddy tells me that I don't know m-m-my right foot from my l-l-left and that I c-c-can't carry a t-tune in a bushel b-b-basket. If I d-don't have to t-t-talk or s-s-sing I'll maybe d-d-do okay. If I w-work r-r-real hard I m-m-might get my f-feet straightened out."

His deep warm laughter rolled out. "That's the spirit. Well, I've got an extra clarinet. I'll bring one over to you and show you how to put it together so you will appear to be playing it. Rehearsal's at 4:15 tomorrow."

He marched out of the room. I remained standing, watching his maroon silk jacket disappear in the distance. From the corner of my eye I noticed that Miss Maupin was watching him too.

There was an explosion of voices around me: "Gee, Rog. You're lucky! *You* get to march with the big kids? Guess there's some advantage to bein' a long drinka' water." Derisive laughter followed. I was used to it.

I folded into my desk in dumb amazement. I had always loved watching the marching band. I knew I'd never be in it because my family couldn't afford to rent an instrument.

I wondered what a clarinet was. I didn't know my instruments. I walked up to Miss Maupin's desk and requested a library pass for during recess. I remembered from my Greek mythology that Orpheus had something to do with music, but I forgot what he played.

Arriving at the library, I headed for the collections of the ancient stories. I found a picture of Orpheus. He was playing something called a lyre. I wondered if a clarinet was anything like that.

Orpheus had to go to the Underworld and hunt for his wife. Between my daddy's beatings and the kids teasing me about my stammer, I felt like I already lived there. If I got real good in music, maybe I could get away from the pain at least sometime.

I leafed through the book and came upon a picture of Pan

playing his pipes. He looked a lot happier than Orpheus. Maybe a clarinet would be something like them.

Before returning to the classroom, I paused at the encyclopedia. There, under "clarinet," I saw it—a long, slender silver instrument. I caught my breath. *I* was going to get to carry one of those? My heart whirled with joy as I walked down the hall. Invisible snare drums cadenced *my* steps.

Sherm Savola had said that I didn't have to play it. But maybe I could learn. My imagination soared. Someday I could play in an orchestra with one of those operas I secretly listened to on Saturday afternoon if my daddy wasn't around and the radio batteries were charged.

The next morning Mr. Savola, every black curl in place, a white rose in the buttonhole of his blue silk jacket, marched into the fifth-grade room with a black case in his hand. He came straight to my desk. Miss Maupin rushed toward me as well. She greeted Mr. Savola warmly and said that she should watch just how one put a clarinet together. If I got into trouble she could help me. Besides, she had given some thought to playing the clarinet herself. The community band which Mr. Savola conducted always needed new players. If she decided to try it, she'd most certainly need some private lessons. Did he give them?

His answering smile let the whole world know that he gave such lessons. Looking into her eyes, he confessed to a woeful shortage of clarinets in the community band. I was momentarily forgotten between them.

Suddenly he remembered the purpose of his visit, and, bending down, he opened the case and set aside the worn copy of *The Smith-Yoder-Bachman Beginning Method for the B-flat Clarinet*. Six silver pieces lay like crown jewels in the burgundy crushed-velvet lining. He instructed me in the order of their assemblage.

As an afterthought, he demonstrated the mounting of the reed on the mouthpiece which he referred to as the instrument's vocal chord. He said, "I showed you how to do that just in case you want to try to make a sound."

That afternoon, I asked the stern faced bus driver, Fritz Minnery, to let me off at the stop nearest my Hermit Uncle John. I wanted him to be the first to know about my latest (and thus far only) triumph.

Both Tiny and Pity Me met me at the edge of the woods. They ran intricate circles and figure eights around me as I hurried to the cabin. I burst through the door, shouting, "Uncle John! Uncle John! Look what I've got!" In my excitement, I completely lost my stammer.

He leaped, startled from his chair where he'd been reading Shakespeare. "I'd prefer y-y-you made a quieter e-e-entrance."

I quickly told him the story of my being chosen to march with the older kids because I was tall.

Uncle John asked with a perfectly straight face, "Were you taught to play whatever is hiding in that fancy black case?"

I had spent all my time on the bus studying *Bachman*. A handsome man from the Paris Conservatory was seated with the instrument positioned correctly. There was a close-up of just how one's lips were to fold around the mouthpiece and its reed. I was to work hard on perfecting what the illustration was trying to teach: something unpronounceable called "embrochure."

I responded with studied casualness, "I'm p-p-pretty sure I can play her."

I carefully assembled the pieces as I'd been taught. I attached the reed to the mouthpiece with the metal straps. I sat in an ancient ladder-back chair in exactly the position prescribed in the picture from the Paris Conservatory: back straight, left foot slightly extended, embrochure firmly around the reed.

I inhaled until my lungs were about to burst and exhaled a mighty breath into the instrument. The resultant sound was like the dying cry of a guinea hen caught in a weasel's teeth. Tiny erupted in a mournful howl, while Pity Me leaped straight into the air and sought refuge in the protective "U" of the dog's paws.

After initial surprise my Hermit Uncle John doubled over in unfamiliar laughter. He gasped, "I-I-I've not heard a s-s-sound like that since the War when the p-piper for a Scottish regiment took a b-b-bullet in his b-b-bags. I've j-just been reading Sh-Sh-Shakespeare's play 'T-T-Twelfth Night.' It begins with D-D-Duke Orsino commanding, 'If music be the food of love, play on.' I'm not sure th-th-that's exactly what h-h-he meant."

He continued to choke back chuckles. Finally he regained his composure enough to assure me, "R-R-Rog, you kn-know I-I-I'm not laughing at *you*. But a skunk and a d-dog and an old m-m-man who've l-l-lived alone as long as w-we have aren't u-u-used to surprises."

Tiny crept forward and shoved her nose into the clarinet's bell. I let forth another blast. She catapulted into her master's arms.

I decided I should read page two of *Bachman* on "Proper Breathing Techniques."

Leaving the instrument with my Hermit Uncle John, I raced across the fields so as not to be late for supper or milking.

I managed to unscramble my feet. Over the next few weeks I marched with the best of the older performers. Initial resentment of having the "stammering kid" around changed to grudging respect as I silently endured the rigorous rehearsals.

I felt I had arrived when I was given a metal music clip shaped like the instrument in the hands of Orpheus. It was even called a lyre. When band music was given out, I was automatically issued a set whether I could play it or not. Sherm Savola seemed to have forgotten all about me as long as I marched about as well as anyone else.

There was one thing Mr. Savola did *not* know about me. I was curious, determined and hungry to find anything which might provide a respite from my father's darknesses.

I began spending every possible moment with my clarinet

and *Bachman*. I worked through every exercise. I would play an open "g" for long periods of time until it mellowed to a point where neither Tiny nor Skippy, my dog, would howl. Soon my tone was as mellow as the whistle of a lone train on a frosty midnight. But nobody knew.

I learned all the fingerings. I would play each note carefully until it seemed to me to rival in quality anything I heard from the more experienced players. But nobody knew.

I spent hours doing finger dexterity exercises: shaking my hands until my fingers completely relaxed, playing imaginary scales while teachers lectured. This was especially true in Pip Pippert's class. He was the history teacher and football coach. In the fall he would outline all the plays for Friday night's game during the morning class. The blackboard would be covered with diagrams which, to the casual passings of the principal, could possibly be mistaken for diagrams of the Napoleonic Wars.

On Monday morning he would analyze Friday's foray with even more elaborate drawings. Everyone except the players and the cheerleaders would sit in glassy-eyed pseudoattention. This left only Tuesday, Wednesday and Thursday to learn about the Dark Ages and the Industrial Revolution. These were subjects fairly obscure in Mr. Pippert's lexicon of knowledge. I kept *Bachman* open on my desk and silently played through exercise after exercise on Mondays and Fridays. I emerged from it all a good clarinet player and an inept historian. But to this point, nobody knew.

One day I heard Mr. Savola say to his departing intermediate clarinet class, "Everybody works at their own speed. All the books for beginners, intermediate and advanced are in my office. Don't hesitate to check out a beginners and look again at your basic skills or grab an advanced and give yourself a little challenge."

I slipped into his office when no one was around and exchanged my beginner's book for an intermediate. Nobody knew.

Soon I began to practice the actual music the band was playing. As I learned the easier pieces, I began to play at a whisper while we marched. And nobody knew.

My daddy didn't find out about the presence of the clarinet for a number of weeks. He didn't mind my coming home on a late bus if I was there in time for milking the cows. He thought I was having trouble with reading and was staying for help.

Sometimes I would sneak the clarinet home in my bookbag and hide it under the foot of my mattress. On occasion I would get off near Uncle John's and spend some time in what increasingly became heavenly hope. Sometimes when the frustration level got real high on a new musical task, Uncle John would stand behind me and rub my back and murmur encouraging sounds until the problem was solved.

One day my parents left for town. I had the clarinet hidden at home. As soon as they were out of the driveway I pulled it from its place of concealment and began to practice. I completely lost myself in the exercises. My fingers flew over the keys.

I didn't hear the immediate return of Mom and Dad. They'd forgotten to take one case of eggs which they were to deliver to the produce station. I suddenly was aware that I was not alone. Skippy, as if expecting the visitation of doom, crept under my bed. I stopped the ripple of notes. Out of the corner of my eye I saw my father standing in my bedroom door, his face a chiseled mask of anger. Behind him stood my frightened mother, helpless to intervene in whatever might happen.

I knew what he was going to do. He'd grab my precious instrument and smash it to the floor and smash *me* to the floor along with it. Without thinking, I began to play strains of a tune I'd heard wafted over the waters from the Six Fat Dutchmen to Shaman's Point many times: "The Clarinet Polka."

My performance was highly flawed, but the contents were recognizable. My father's face relaxed and he exploded, "I'll be damned. The kid knows how to play that thing, and he's playing something good rather than that stupid grand opera stuff I keep catching him listening to on Saturday afternoons."

He turned, bowed to my mother and said in a courtly manner, "May I have this dance?"

He grabbed her and they did a wild polka around the living room. Skippy slid out from in under the bed, stared in stark amazement, then ran in and out around them leaping and barking. My mother buried her head in my father's shoulder and wept for sheer joy.

I continued to play the only phrase I knew over and over again until they collapsed on the worn living room couch with the broken springs. I stopped playing. I heard him say to her softly, "Mary, I wish we could have danced forever."

Six hours later he descended into a terrible darkness. We both felt the whip of his anger.

However, that unique moment must have burned into his subconscious. He never complained about my music as long as he lived.

I didn't let on to Mr. Savola that I was learning to play the instrument. He merely watched me march in the various formations. He even commented that I was doing a good job. He was glad he'd chosen me. He would never know, I thought, at least for a long, long time.

One day, I betrayed my own secret. The three others in the clarinet section were seniors. They were off on a special outing. I was alone. Mr. Savola announced the march "Under the Double Eagle." I loved the clarinet part and had practiced it a lot.

We began marching down the field. I was simply whispering the part over the reed. I was transported by the whirling sounds around me. I let the solo ring out loud and clear and almost in tune.

Mr. Savola stopped the high-stepping ensemble. He spoke to me very firmly: "Roger, will you step up here to the front of the band?"

I did as I was asked, certain that I'd had no business being there, that I'd played the music badly and that thunderbolts from heaven would rain down upon us all because of my transgressions.

He continued, "Now, Rog—would you play that last little passage one more time?"

It was very simple and very showy. I finished it. There was scattered applause from the onlookers, the first such approbation I'd ever received. Mr. Savola looked at me long and hard and finally commented softly, "I thought you were just carrying that instrument around in order to fill a marching position. How did you ever figure it out?"

"The *B-B-Bachman* b-b-books sir."

"If you've learned all that on your own, then wait and see what kind of a player we'll have when you've had a few private lessons from *me*."

And private lessons I did have. They gave me more cause to practice for hours on end, trying to lose myself in a world beyond my father's anger.

The year was a progression of bake sales and bean suppers as everybody was involved in some way or another to raise money for the new band uniforms. We hoped to have them by Memorial Day so we'd close off the year in splendor.

They arrived in early May. They were beautiful, patterned as they were after the dress uniforms of West Point cadets. Mine fit perfectly. I could hardly wait for the great day to arrive.

After school that day I headed for my Hermit Uncle John's to share the great news with him. When I walked into his cabin he sensed my excitement. He laid down his Bible. He went into the kitchen for milk and fresh-baked oatmeal cookies with which to calm me down.

My mission was to convince him to come and see us when we marched and played in the Pheasant Valley Memorial Cemetery on Decoration Day. After all, he and my dad had ancestors there. Shouldn't he bring a few peonies in a mason jar to put on his father's grave?

He reluctantly promised to walk across the fields for the

great event. I was pleased.

The morning of Memorial Day dawned overcast and chilly. We moved into formation outside the gates. On a signal from the American Legion Post commander the snare drums would begin a gentle cadence. The wrought iron gates were thrown open. The signal came. We moved with stately grace as we played "The Funeral March" from *Aida*.

The first person I noticed was my Hermit Uncle John. When he saw me he burst into tears and disappeared.

I was worried about him. We played through all the necessary pieces. Then we disbanded under a flag-draped oak tree. I went in search of my lost uncle.

I guessed that he might have followed my suggestion and brought some flowers for his parents' graves. As I neared the Robbennolt plot, I heard a strange sound. I followed it.

I found my Hermit Uncle John crouched behind his father's tombstone sobbing his heart out. I rushed to him, knelt down beside him and held him.

"Uncle John. Uncle John. What's the m-m-matter, Uncle J-J-John?"

The first words I could hear were, "S-S-Soldier b-b-boys. S-S-Soldier boys. Why d-did they have t-t-to make you l-l-look like soldier boys?"

I remained silent. Between sobs he continued: "The cemetery's filled with flags t-t-today, as is every graveyard in America. W-W-We remember all the b-boys that g-g-got killed in every w-w-war ever fought."

Then, with fire in his eyes, he continued, "How could anybody make you look like soldier boys? W-W-We come here to remember those who d-died in the m-m-mud of faraway places. Yet we even d-dress our b-b-band so that they l-l-look like soldier b-b-boys. That makes b-b-bein' a killer seem glamorous."

He burst into sobs again. When he caught his breath, he turned, looked me in the eyes and put a hand on my shoulder. He said, "R-R-Rog, the other day when you came to see me

I was reading the Gospel of Matthew. Jesus' disciples had just come to him. He told them, among other things, 'Blessed are the peacemakers for they shall be called the children of God.' Please make me a p-p-promise. Even th-th-though you're d-d-dressed like a soldier, always l-look for a b-b-better way to peace. I want you to be a child of God as surely as those disciples."

I was crying too. I answered, "I'll always t-t-try, Uncle John. That's a p-p-promise. I'll always t-t-try."

And I always have.

Dear Gletha,

My Hermit Uncle John cried today. I haven't told you, but I'm carrying a clarinet with the big kids in the band. Our uniforms make us look like soldiers.

When he saw me, he cried because it reminded him of the war where all his friends were killed. I held him the way you used to hold me. It seemed to help. I'm glad my daddy wasn't there 'cause he says that real men and boys don't cry.

Did I ever make you cry? I hope not.

Love,

Roger

Dear Rogee,

You made me cry a lot. But that's okay. Folks who really care deeply will cry for and with one another.

Always remember that tears are one of the best safety valves God gifted us with. Also remember that it's not only women who cry or men who cry. It's people who cry.

Love,

Gletha

A MEMORABLE THANKSGIVING

I watched bitterly as the scene unfolded twice a day. Dad headed for the henyard morning and evening. With wings flapping and a trumpeting forth of hoarse welcoming honks, the great gander greeted him. Dad reached into his pocket for a handful of shelled corn. The huge bird daintily nibbled the kernels from the palm of his hand.

The gander stretched his incredibly long neck up toward my father. He scratched the enormous fowl beneath its beak. Its neck began to move sinuously like a cobra responding to a fakir's flute.

Dad knelt on the ground, oblivious to the fowlyard manure, and extended his arms. The gander moved forward and nestled against him, extending his wings as if hungering for an embrace from his human friend.

I stood there hungering for an embrace from my father as well. Hugs seldom came. I was more apt to be slapped to the earth as the troubled man descended into his frequent darknesses.

Sometimes when he was in the depth of his mental illness he would desert his usual rocking chair and sit for hours beneath the weeping willow on the edge of Specter Slough. His barnyard companion would appear at his side. Dad would put an arm over his feathered crony and stare blankly out over the distant fields.

The bird had been hatched in the reeds on the slough shore. My dad, when he was out of a darkness, loved to watch the world come alive in the spring. On one occasion he reported that new goslings were paddling in the shallow water.

In a rare gesture of togetherness, he invited me to join in a journey across the fields to observe the newborns at the pond's edge. We sat silently beneath the willow's greening fronds. Five goslings floated lazily on the sunlit water under the watchful eye of the matronly goose. Four clustered together. One paddled alone, circling its siblings.

Suddenly, the lone innocent ball of water-borne fluff exploded toward its peers, slashing them apart. There was an outburst of fear-filled, high-pitched peeping. The marauder swam unconcernedly away, scooping up an occasional water bug on his passage.

The goose hit the water in a flash. She drove her offending youngster to the shore and pinioned him under her wing while the remainder of the family regained its watery composure.

My father was doubled over with laughter. He turned to me and choked out, "Ain't that one a cheeky little devil? We're going to have a real show right here on our pond."

We returned almost daily to the scene. The pond family became so accustomed to our presence that they paid us little heed.

Dad's darknesses were less frequent when there was something in the world that captured his complete attention. The maturation of the feisty gosling fascinated him.

The mother goose was driven to distraction by her unruly offspring. He grew twice as fast as the other babies, probably because he overpowered them completely when anything edible appeared. Soon bloody scabs from his constant pecking could be seen on various parts of their bodies. My sympathies were with the victims. I understood completely how they felt in the midst of familial abuse.

After a particularly vicious incident, the mother goose grabbed the attacker by the slender neck, dragged it to shore and held it to the ground with an enormous webbed foot. My dad laughed so loud that the goose turned and stared at the source of the unwelcome sound. I thought I detected a note of scorn in her eyes as she stared at the insensitive human who made no attempt to understand her predicament.

A month later he began putting corn in his pocket before our expeditions to the slough. He would snap a kernel into the shallow water. The object of his affection would drive the other goslings away before retrieving the gift.

As time went on, Dad began flipping kernels on the shore in a pattern which brought the fast-growing little fowl closer and closer to our post under the willow. A routine developed. Before picking up the corn, the young gander would dance in triumph and warning around the bit of food, flapping his wings and emitting a raw sound from his immature throat that registered somewhere between a honk, a crow and a cackle. Then he would devour the gift as if he'd just been given the caviar of goosedom.

One evening Dad raised a question over dinner. "I wonder what we should name that scrappy little gander?"

Mom suggested, "Why not 'Goosey, Goosey?'"

He responded sharply, "That's a stupid name. You've never even seen my friend."

Mother retreated into her usual teary silence.

I knew what I wanted to call it. Its rightful name was a seven letter word beginning with "B" which my father often screamed at me. However, Mom preferred that it not be spoken in her presence.

Having finished his fried chicken, mashed potatoes with chicken-foot gravy and two pieces of rhubarb pie, Dad retreated to the next room to read "Grit," the weekly newspaper popular in our neighborhood.

A few minutes later I approached him to borrow the paper's second section which contained the continuing Western novel. He was staring at a picture when a slow smile spread across his face.

An evil-faced, long-necked young actor stared back. He was dressed in a Roman toga. His arms were raised in triumph. One hand contained a dagger. The text informed us that Mr. Raymond Halliwell was touring the country as Brutus in a production of William Shakespeare's "Julius Caesar."

"Brutus," mused my father. "Brutus. You know, our young gander looks a bit like that fellah right there. That's what we're going to call him: Brutus."

The next day the word "brute" appeared on my school spelling list. I decided the gander had been aptly named.

The relationship between Dad and Brutus deepened. Soon the young bird was eating from his hand at pondside. The next step was inevitable. Dad began to drop kernels of corn along the path from slough to barnyard. Brutus followed us happily home.

His role and character were immediately established. He marched over to the chicken feeder. He drove the resident hens roughly away, awed the guineas and cowed the roosters into submission. He gorged himself. Then he waddled back to the pond.

Brutus took up permanent residency. My father was delighted. My mother was horrified. She was sure the chickens would stop laying in the light of the hysteria in the henyard. My father defended the presence of his new friend: "As mean as that gander is to the rest of the world 'cept me, there won't be a weasel or a raccoon that will be able to get near the henhouse. Maybe he can do a better job than the kid's worthless dog."

This was a gross overstatement, but it silenced my mother. It didn't take much of a word from my father to do that.

The gander's reign of terror stretched beyond the environs of the barn. He began brutal attacks on my dog, Skippy, and me. He would crouch quietly in the hedgerow. As Skippy went in endless pursuit of gophers and field mice, Brutus would burst from his hiding place and draw blood from the back of the unsuspecting dog through his ferocious pecking.

Skippy would tear up to the house, yipping mournfully as he sought refuge under the front steps. He would curl up on my feet if I were available.

My own encounters with the ravening bird were equally painful. My daddy was dead set against play. Somehow, he managed to communicate his attitude to Brutus. Occasionally, if Dad were in town, I'd sneak a celebratory moment. My favorite pleasure was to kneel in my Radio Flyer red wagon, push off with my right leg, pull it in and coast down the long gentle slope between the house and the barn.

Brutus had telepathic powers. Whenever I planned such a descent, the gander would hide in the thick lilac bushes at the side of the house. Halfway down the slope I would feel a sharp pain in my posterior. Then I would hear the hiss and the triumphant honk and feel at least three more sharp pecks to my butt.

Occasionally, as I struggled to seat myself in the moving vehicle and fight off the attack, I would lose my balance and topple into the dirt. He would jump atop me and beat at me with his wings. Then he would return victorious to his kingdom of egg layers.

I would sometimes join Skippy under the front steps. Together we would plot the demise of the demon gander.

When Thanksgiving approached, I was sure that Brutus' fate was sealed. My mother always traded four guinea hens for a turkey with Millicent Filliber who lived three farms west. However, it had been a terrible year for Millicent. Coccidiosis, a near fatal intestinal parasite, had gained a hold on her turkey flock, wiping out most of her birds.

At dinner the day before Thanksgiving Mom broached the subject of what she could roast special for the festive day. The economy had been awful. Everybody was feeling poor. We couldn't afford to buy a turkey from the poultry processing plant in Pheasant Hollow.

My dad remained silent. I decided to venture my fantastic idea. "B-B-Brutus is real f-fat from all the corn h-h-he eats.

He'd be r-real tender. Why d-d-don't we let M-M-Mom roast him."

Dad flew into a rage. "That's just the sort of dumb fool idea I've come to expect from you. You'd just love to roast one of the only friends I've got in the whole damn world. You'd also leave the henyard unprotected."

He turned on my mother. "You want something special to put on the table for Thanksgiving? Well, by God, I'll get you something special to roast."

He leaped from the table and grabbed his shotgun. He threw on his red plaid hunting jacket and stormed out the door, slamming it loudly. Brutus gave a warning honk in response to the sudden sound. My mother paled with fright. We never knew what he was going to do next, especially if he had a gun in his hand. The cock's tail on the barntop weather vane, the steel paddles on the windmill and the flag on the mailbox all were marred with bullet holes.

I raised a question with my mother: "Mom, d-d-d-do you th-th-think he's h-h-heading into a d-d-darkness?"

"No. He'll stay watchful. He wouldn't want to take a chance that we would do anything to his gander."

Tears rolled down her cheeks as she continued, "I just wish he cared as much for us as he does for his horses and Brutus."

Winter darkness descended early. As I carried in pails of milk from the barn, I saw him, shadowed by the full moon, coming over the snow-powdered field.

I returned to the barn for the final pail. He stepped into the building after me. In the soft yellow light of the suspended lantern, I saw that he carried, slung over his shoulder, the lifeless carcass of a fat raccoon. I shuddered. Skippy nosed the dead beast.

My father instructed me, "Finish carrying in the milk. After supper we'll dress out the raccoon. We'll have the best Thanksgiving dinner you ever tasted."

He took a handful of corn from the horse manger, paused at the chicken coop where Brutus had a special perch in the corner and celebrated the safety of his dearest friend with a particularly intense outpouring of affection.

The house was filled with the cinnamony smell of fresh-baked pumpkin pie. It had competition from the odor of sage rising from a large wooden bowl filled with the dressing ready to stuff whatever my father returned with.

He took off his coat. His face was flushed with the joy of the hunt and the winter cold. My mother asked, "Well, Frank, did you have any luck?"

He nodded.

"What am I going to roast for tomorrow? A brace of squirrels? A jackrabbit? A pair of ducks?"

I stared at her to see her response when he made his announcement.

He answered, "We're going to have the most delicious meat for Thanksgiving dinner you've ever eaten. I shot us a nice fat raccoon that's been stealing corn from the corn crib all fall since that worthless Skippy is no good as a watchdog."

Hearing his name mentioned in that tone of voice, my dog slunk out from under the table where I slipped him scraps and into my bedroom where he curled up on the raccoonskin rug at the foot of my bed. Dad would occasionally make rugs from the hides of the friendly beasts. This was the first time he'd suggested we eat one.

My mother stared at her food. I turned my attention to the half-eaten hard fried eggs covered with catsup on my plate. A wave of nausea arose at the prospect of tomorrow's dinner.

Seeing the expressions on our faces, Dad started to laugh. "Get those sour looks off your faces. You eat bacon, don't you? Well, a raccoon is a lot cleaner than a pig. Once I get it dressed out, you can stuff it and roast it just like a turkey except you put it on a rack so the fat can run off good. Now, kid, finish your supper and come out to the barn, and I'll teach you to skin it out."

I choked down the remainder of my food to avoid his angry insistence that I clean my plate. We put on our coats. I reluctantly followed him to the barn with Skippy at my heels. In the distance Brutus honked gleefully.

Dad struck a match and lighted the hanging lantern. He placed a wide, thick board across a manger to use as a butcher block. He took out his razor sharp hunting knife. He showed me where to slice through the skin from each leg and down the center of the belly. I did not move fast enough.

He demanded sharply, "Give me that knife. You're slower than molasses in January."

With a hunter's practiced hand he quickly made additional incisions and slipped off the skin. I tried to avoid looking at the smiling mask which had mocked me from the walnut tree on autumn evenings. My dad carved out the bean-shaped scent glands from beneath each leg. In moments he had gutted the beast, removed its head and sliced off the winter fat gained from our corn.

Dad handed the freshly butchered carcass to me. I took it gingerly. It was heavier than I anticipated. It slipped from my hands to the straw-covered floor.

He slapped me 'side the head and shouted, "When are you going to learn not to be so damned clumsy? Now, pick it up and take it to your ma. Tell her to stuff it just like she would a turkey and set it in the back entry for the night. I'm going to stay here and throw down a little more hay for the cattle."

He disappeared up the worn wooden ladder into the haymow. I carried the carcass through the moonlit night. I paused by the open door to the henhouse, closed my eyes and imagined that I was bearing the body of the butchered Brutus. As if the gander understood my every thought, he threw me a taunting honk from within.

I entered the kitchen. My mother was finishing the supper dishes. She turned, saw the dressed raccoon and caught her breath. She reluctantly reached for it. I put it in her hands.

At that moment our ring—a short and a long and a short and a long—blared out from the wall phone. The bell was extra-loud since Dad had just changed the batteries. She jumped at the sound, and the carcass slipped to the floor a second time. She rushed to the phone. I retrieved the raccoon and filled the empty dishpan with water to wash it off.

My mother was holding the receiver away from her ear. All the way to the kitchen I could hear the strident voice of her cousin, Philomel, booming from the earpiece.

"Mary, can you hear me? There's some phone lines down from the heavy wind in these parts."

"Yes, Philomel. I can hear you fine."

Could she ever! Philomel and her husband Francis lived eleven miles south of us. At the volume she was speaking I'd probably be able to hear her voice wafted over the still air of the winter night if I just stepped outside.

"Well, Mary," Philomel continued to shout, "how would you like some unexpected company for Thanksgiving?"

"I thought you and Francis were going to his folks' in Dakota."

"They just now called. It's blizzarding to beat the band out there. They said we'd be fools to try. So I just said to Francis, 'I'm going to call up Frank and Mary and invite ourselves.' "

She burst out in a gale of what Dad always described as "Philomel's horselaugh." Mom held the receiver a few more inches from her ear. Skippy went on alert.

Mother responded, "Why, that's fine, Philomel. We're always glad to share, but...."

She was not allowed to finish her sentence. Philomel cut her off with, "Mary, I just knew you'd understand. Besides, I'd rather eat with you. You make the best turkey this side of heaven."

"But Philomel...."

She was cut off again at the verbal pass by Philomel. "Now, Mary, don't you say another word. I'll bring some of my special rose hip jelly to spread on your scrumptious cornbread. You are baking a big pan of your scrumptious cornbread, aren't you?"

Before mother could answer, Philomel swept on: "It just

wouldn't be Thanksgiving without a b-i-g pan of your scrumptious cornbread. And of course I'll bring a quart jar of my prize-winning green-tomato preserves. Well, we'll see you about two o'clock tomorrow. 'Bye now."

In one fell swoop Philomel, as an uninvited guest, had established the menu and set the time. She purposefully clashed her receiver into its cradle, sending a bolt of metallic sound slicing through our nervous systems. Mother quietly replaced her instrument with a sense of resignation. Another person had taken control of her life.

When we had recovered, Mom and I looked at each other. We began to grin, then chuckle; then we burst into a united, unaccustomed belly laugh. Our minds both conjured up the image of the overpowering Philomel and her frail Francis partaking of raccoon on the following feast day.

Philomel and Francis Fackenthall were my mother's shirttail relations. They'd invited themselves to Thanksgiving dinner the last six years. Dad had made it clear last year that it was the final sacrificial meal. We all agreed. We rejoiced when they announced plans to go to Dakota, or "Dakoty" as Francis always pronounced it.

If there was one thing I dreaded more about the morrow than munching on raccoon, it was my annual encounter with the prize-winning green-tomato preserves. Eleven years ago Philomel had been awarded a third-place ribbon in the condiments division at the Hawkhill County Fair. Ever since, she had dreamed of patenting the recipe (or "receep" as it was known in her circle) and distributing it worldwide in jars with gold labels reading: "PHILOMEL'S PHAMOUS GREEN-TOMATO PRESERVES."

She had recently commented to my mother that she had hated her first name until recently when she decided that it went right well with PHAMOUS.

When fall arrived, she would go down on her knees and pray for a light frost. She'd dash to the garden and gather the unripe fruit from the frozen tomato vines. She'd mush them together with her secret collage of spices and allow them to ferment slightly before putting them in blue Kerr mason jars which made the contents appear even less appetizing.

Francis confided to my mother that on occasion a jar would explode in the root cellar. Great shards of glass would stick in the cellar door. The inherent danger gave him pause. It was like playing Russian roulette to perform a simple task like going down and getting a few rutabagas for the chickens from the bin in the corner.

Each Thanksgiving dinner found her standing at the head of the table doling out a large dollop of sickly green mush on each plate without consulting anyone.

After a long time, Dad came in from the barn.

I said, "You must have brought down a lot of hay."

"Naw. I decided to scrape the raccoon hide and nail it to a stretcher board so it can dry real good."

Mom said hesitantly, "I've got some bad news, Frank. The Dakotas are snowed in. Philomel and Francis have invited themselves for Thanksgiving dinner again."

Dad was silent for a long moment. Then he stepped toward the sink where Mom and I had begun to stuff the raccoon. He started to grin. We all followed suit. The progress from grin to chuckle to belly laugh progressed quickly. In an unprecedented action the three of us collapsed into each other's arms cackling uproariously. For a moment all anger was assuaged and we were together.

Mom finally gasped out, "She said they were coming because I roast the best turkey this side of heaven."

The whole family longed to get revenge on her one way or another. Perhaps tomorrow would bring the opportunity.

I chopped a few more onions for the dressing. Dad rolled up his sleeves and began stuffing the rich mixture of bread, black walnuts, apples, raisins, onions and sage into the cavity of the carcass. This was the only time in my life I would ever see him do anything like this.

When the beast was firmly stuffed, Mom sewed up the

stomach seam. We lifted it in triumph to the roaster. All hesitation over the gastronomic niceties of the central item on tomorrow's menu were obscured by the shared joy of Philomel's comeuppance at the Thanksgiving table. I decided that I might have something to be thankful about after all.

Dad slipped to the root cellar and returned with three Greenings from the apple barrel, each wrapped in an individual page from an outdated Montgomery Ward catalogue. He washed the apples, halved them and fastened them with skewers into the open place where the head had been.

While he completed the task, I became mesmerized by one of the catalogue pages. The company was starting something called a book club. The first selection being offered to subscribers was *The Robe* by Lloyd C. Douglas. I dreamed of being rich someday and being able to belong to a book club. The advertisement pictured a Roman in a toga. I was reminded of Brutus. I guess I was glad I hadn't gotten my way to have him served up on a platter.

My dad returned from carrying the roaster to the back entry. He stood over me without my being aware of him. He interrupted my reverie with, "Losin' yourself in books ag'in, eh? When are you going to learn that books don't need no plowman."

"Yeah, but this plowman needs books."

It slipped out before I thought. I waited for the usual blow to fall. He simply looked at me quietly, smiled and said, "Well, forget the books until after tomorrow when we make a new woman out of Philomel."

I awoke early in a grey foggy dawn. My parents were stirring below me. My father was building a fire in the cookstove so that the oven temperature would be right for the roast.

We lingered an unusually long time over breakfast. Ma rose from the table. She mixed up a large batch of her "simply scrumptious cornbread." Dad and I headed for the barn where the cows were lowing in discomfort, waiting to be milked. He stopped for a time to commune with Brutus.

Preparations for the impending celebration proceeded quietly. A crocheted tablecloth was spread on the living room table. Its pineapple design was accented by the dark wood. It was soon ornamented with settings of 1847 Rogers Bros. silver plate which had been slowly acquired over the years with Betty Crocker coupons.

The cornbread was stirred together, potatoes peeled and the milk and flour mixed in readiness for the gravy. A red glass bowl which had come as a premium in a ten pound bag of oatmeal was placed in readiness for the proper display of the prize-winning green-tomato preserves.

When Dad returned from the barn, we all agreed that the smells wafting from the oven rivaled those of other holidays. Mom had obviously outdone herself on the dressing.

Two o'clock approached. Our conspiratorial excitement mounted. All was in readiness. Even Skippy made special preparations. He dragged the raccoonskin rug from the floor at the foot of my bed into the living room and under the table so he could curl up in comfort while awaiting special tidbits slipped to him during the meal.

Brutus honked a high note, warning us of an approaching vehicle. Within minutes a 1924 Model A turned cautiously into the driveway. The ignition was turned off, and the car coasted down the slope to a parking place by the barn. Francis liked to "save a little gas" at every opportunity.

Philomel emerged slowly from the car. The multitude of brightly colored scarves in which she ever bedecked herself caught the breeze and assisted in propelling her up the hill with increasing speed toward our waiting family. She was not slowed down by a limp caused by the huge bunion which protruded through the hole slit in the leather of her worn left shoe.

She engulfed my mother in a bosomy, scarf-smothered embrace. I stepped away to escape a similar fate.

The emaciated Francis minced slowly after her, staring at

the scene of welcome through tiny, round gold rimmed glasses perched on the end of a long nose. His huge, unbuckled galoshes clomped ominously on the frozen ground.

In his left hand he carried a basket extended gingerly as far away from his body as possible, as if he momentarily expected an explosion. It contained the promised jelly and preserves.

The guests entered the house. Their coats were stacked on the bed in my parents' room. Philomel retrieved a few scarves to wrap around her neck "just in case there should be a little draft."

She swept into the kitchen and picked up her jar of green-tomato preserves. She moved toward the special red dish. She attempted to unscrew the lid as she went. Failing, she handed the jar to Francis who was wedged into a corner by the stove, vainly attempting to warm his frail frame after the wintry journey.

He feebly grasped the lid to no avail. He waved the offending jar at me. I swaggered over, grabbed the container and gave the lid a mighty wrench. It loosened. Bubbles began rushing toward the top of the jar.

As I turned the lid the final screw, it rocketed from the jar, knocking a hole in the low lying ceiling's plaster. The top quarter of the contents sprayed out onto the hot stove. The small room was engulfed in thick smoke that smelled like a moonshiner's still in a forest fire.

Philomel fanned the smoke with her scarves. Doors were opened. Order was restored. She grabbed the jar from my startled hands.

She shouted sharply, "Clumsy boy! You've gone and wasted about half the jar!"

She turned the jar upside down. The remaining preserves plopped glopulously into the red bowl. I whispered to my father, "It sounds and looks like fresh cow dung at apple time."

He momentarily buried his face in my hair to suppress the snickers. My father had touched me nonviolently the second time in two days. Perhaps the Fackenthall's visit had a special purpose after all.

Philomel continued sadly, "Well, I guess I'll just have to serve smaller portions." There was a general sigh of relief.

Mom announced that everything was about ready. We should all sit down and drink our glasses of canned blueberry juice which began each festive meal. Francis left his corner by the stove and slithered through the narrow passage between table edge and wall. He sat by a window after momentarily entangling himself in its lace curtain. It seemed like Francis was always partially disappearing into whatever he found himself next to.

Having finished his juice, Dad headed to the kitchen to "carve the beast." Philomel and Francis missed the implications of his statement.

Philomel interrupted his leave-taking with, "I want everybody to stop where they are so's we can have a bit of prayer."

The prayer was wide-ranging, including all the little children: yellow, black and white. Its major thrust seemed to be thanking the Almighty that we were among the fortunate few to savor one of Millicent Filliber's surviving fowls.

Mom brought in a tray piled high with her scrumptious cornbread. Francis grabbed the two biggest pieces. Philomel glared at him.

Mom carried in potatoes and gravy and a huge bowl of dressing. The Fackenthalls waited for nobody as they heaped their plates high. Philomel then flitted around the table, gracing everybody's plate with prize-winning preserves. I put a little of the pungent sauce on a corner of cornbread and held it down to Skippy just to see what he would do. He left the room, climbed up on my bed and curled down on my pillow.

Philomel purred, "I'm gettin' so comfortable at your table, Mary, I've took my shoes off, and I'm enjoying wiggling my toes in the fur of that little raccoonskin rug Skippy dragged under the table. I've heard tell that raccoon oil is real good for bunions."

She shouted toward the kitchen, "Frank, when we was here

last Thanksgiving, I told you I had my heart set on a cute little rug like this one under my feet right now. Have you done anything about it?"

Dad responded, "As soon as we've finished eatin', I'll show you just what I've done about it."

He entered with a gold-edged china platter decorated with briar roses. It was the only thing he possessed that belonged to his grandmother. It was stacked with thinly sliced meat.

I had to admit the forest creature smelled wonderful roasted. I looked across the table at Francis. A thin river of saliva ran from the left corner of his mouth.

Dad stacked succulent white slices atop Philomel's mountain of dressing. She picked up a morsel with her fingers and tasted it. She nearly swooned with delight.

"Mary," she exploded, "you've just gone and outdid yourself with this turkey."

The three of us looked at one another conspiratorially. In unison we forked a bite of meat and placed it in our mouths as if we were receiving the Sacrament. We found it good.

As the meal progressed, Mom found it impossible to remain in her chair. She circled the table like a border collie with a herd of sheep. She was at everyone's elbow, anticipating their every need. At one point she dashed to the root cellar for a pint of bread-and-butter pickles, without which no festive meal should be served.

In spite of warnings to "save room for the pie" Philomel and Francis had four helpings of everything. Finally, Francis sank back in his chair and dozed behind the veil of curtain, on occasion emitting a dried-up little snore.

Dad pushed his chair back and said, "So's we have a break before dessert, I've got something to show you, Philomel."

He stepped to the porch where he had leaned the stretched skin earlier in the day. He carried it over to her. She squealed with delight. Francis jumped in his chair and then peered embarrassedly through his little round glasses.

"Frank, you are just too sweet for words, making this just

for me."

She stroked her cheek against the soft fur.

She continued, "I do declare, all this excitement's made me a bit hungry again. The meat platter's empty so I'll just slip out to the kitchen and slice me a wee tad more. Now, Mary, since you've finally set to eat, don't you hop. I'm family and I can help myself."

The three of us froze in anticipation.

In a few moments she returned. Her plate was empty. She had a strange look on her face. In a tight little voice she queried, "Have I gone and missed the fact that Millicent Filliber's developed a new breed of turkey with four legs? Or did you serve up a suckling pig to surprise us? What was that we jest et?"

Dad said in an overly calm voice, "Now, Philomel, don't go flustering yourself. You've been sayin' for the last hour that it's some of the best meat you ever et. Well, till about eight o'clock last night that meat you liked s-o-o much was stealing corn from my corncrib while walking around inside that lovely present I fixed for you."

Philomel blanched whiter than one of Tillie Ingebretsen's prize sheets. She flung herself out the back door and dashed shoeless through the skift of snow with scarves flying toward the two-seater at the edge of the tree line.

Fortunately for us, the wind blew the sound of her dinner loss across the field toward the Tarrunder's place.

Francis was lolling limply in his chair with his eyes scrunched shut. I didn't know if he'd fainted or was simply escaping back into sleep from that which he didn't really understand.

When Philomel returned, she passed silently through our midst to the bedroom. Removing her rouge from her purse she flamed her cheeks. She turned, robed herself in her winter coat and arranged her array of scarves.

She said sharply, "Francis!"

He leaped to his feet and skittered kitchenward to retrieve

his galoshes. He quickly donned his sheepskin overcoat. She pulled on her bunion-slitted slippers.

Philomel spoke no other words. She drew herself to her full six-foot height and began to process from the room with unmatchable theatrical dignity. Suddenly she turned. I was sure she was going to cast a curse on all future generations of our family. Instead she gracefully swept up the board with the raccoonskin stretched upon it.

Then she and her silent husband simply faded into the gathering darkness. I stood on the porch and watched as the frail Francis huddled over the steering wheel while Philomel attempted to crank the ancient auto. She couldn't seem to turn the cold motor. She leaned weakly over the radiator. She appeared to be crying.

I couldn't stand it any longer. I'd cranked the car for Dad many times in all kinds of weather. I swaggered to the front of their vehicle.

"H-H-Here, Ph-Ph-Philomel. Let me try it."

Wordlessly, she handed me the crank. Throwing all my strength into it, I managed to turn it over once—then twice—then a third time. The engine caught.

I returned the crank to her. As I walked away from the sputtering car, I saw Francis adjusting the levers on the steering wheel with one hand while rolling down the window with the other.

He beckoned me over and held out his hand. I took off my mitten to shake hands with him. He pressed a warm dime into my palm.

He stepped on the gas. The vehicle backfired loudly. It began to move. As the vehicle exploded into life, Brutus honked a triumphant chorus of thanksgiving that he had not met his demise on this waning holiday.

I went back into the living room. Mom cleared the table. Dad lighted the kerosene lamp. I headed for the kitchen to bring on the pumpkin pie.

Dad started to chuckle. Mom's eyes sparkled. I laughed

outright. Together we relived the subterfuge as we heaped fresh whipped cream upon the fragrant dessert. We would certainly never have to worry about their joining us ever again.

Yet, somewhere beneath the hilarity lurked a sense that something had been destroyed. We didn't quite know what.

When we finished the pie, Dad got up and riddled up the desert dishes. Mom almost fainted in surprise.

Taking advantage of the strange calm, I queried, "Uncle John's probably been alone all day. Could I take him a slice of meat and a piece of pie?"

As if to assuage his nagging discomfort over our mischief of the afternoon, Dad assented. Mom took my school lunchbox and filled it with generous portions of raccoon, dressing and pie.

Dad lighted a smoky lantern for me. I stepped into the moonless night. The light scarcely penetrated the darkness. It cast shadows which quickly became avenging phantoms. My feet sprouted wings as I sped across the fields.

I burst into the cabin. Uncle John was sitting beneath his reading lamp, his Bible in his hands. He leaped to his feet, scattering the book, the ever present dog and the pet skunk. Before he could say a word, I blurted out, "I brought you some dinner fresh from our table. Dad shot a raccoon for Thanksgiving."

Uncle John looked surprised and asked, "How did he happen to do that?"

"W-W-Well it was mostly for old Brutus' sake. Ma and I wanted to roast him, b-but Dad wouldn't hear of it. S-S-So he k-k-killed a raccoon. It r-really isn't too bad a-tastin'."

Uncle John questioned, "Didn't I see Philomel and Francis Fackenthall's car drive down the road past Kahler's Korner? I thought it was a mite early for folks to be leavin' that had just eaten a mighty feast and probably shoulda' been nappin'."

The mere thought of the events earlier in the day sent me into a paroxysm of uncontrolled giggles. I gave him a blow-by-blow account of the hilarious Thanksgiving events when the odd woman and her skinny husband, who had no business being at our place anyhow since they weren't supposed to have been invited, really got their comeuppance.

For the first time I noticed something strange. As I elaborated on the various incidents with the excess of a burgeoning storyteller, I noticed that my Hermit Uncle John seemed to be retreating deeper and deeper into himself.

I finished. There was a l-o-n-g silence. Then he spoke so softly that I had to strain to hear him. "So you played the best joke in the world on 'em by feedin' 'em raccoon. You think you've driven them away so they'll never come back.

"Well, let me tell you a little something about them folk. They're probably some of the most alone folk in the whole world. They had a little girl a long time ago. Named her Diana 'cause she was born when the moon was full. Philomel has always been into things like that.

"Diana died of the diphtheria when she was two. They tried to have another child. It died at birth. They tried six more times. Each baby died at birth. Finally they got told to stop tryin'. Some doctor decided that something was wrong between them in their blood that kept the babies from seein' the world alive."

I began to squirm inside. I could tell where this story was going.

He continued, "I hear tell they've got a little private graveyard in the corner of their cherry orchard. Francis made a bench, and they've been seen sittin' there in all kinds of weather and at all hours of the day and night. They come off to everyone as real odd. But, they need folk like the rest of us do."

There was a catch in his voice.

He took the box of food and placed it on the table. Tiny sat on the floor with her nose pointed toward the pungent sliced raccoon.

I blew out the smoky lantern. Uncle John put an arm around my shoulder and drew me toward his chair. He picked up the Bible and sat down. I curled up at his feet, my head on his knee. Pity Me, the skunk, slipped into my lap. Tiny gave up her quest for roast raccoon and shaped herself around my feet.

Uncle John said softly, "I want to plant a couple of things deep inside you. They're words from this Bible. You've had a lot of fun at the expense of Philomel and Francis. Well, a long time ago Jesus spoke some words to folk who were tempted to put down others. They come from Matthew's Gospel:

> Judge not, that ye be not judged. For with what judgment ye judge, ye shall be judged. And with what measure ye mete, it shall be measured to you again.
>
> And why beholdest thou the mote that is in thy brother's eye, but considerest not the beam that is in thine own eye?
>
> Or how wilt thou say to thy brother, 'Let me pull the mote out of thine eye'; and, behold, a beam is in thine own eye?
>
> Thou hypocrite, first cast the beam out of thine own eye, and then shalt thou see clearly to cast the mote out of thy brother's eye.

"There's some other words written by an old man to special friends just before he died. His name was John, same as mine."

Uncle John read quietly:

> For this is the message that ye heard from the beginning, that we should love one another. Not as Cain, who was of that wicked one, and slew his brother. And wherefore slew he him? Because his own works were evil and his brother's righteous.
>
> Marvel not, my brethren, if the world hate you. We know that we have passed from death unto life because we love the brethren. He that loveth not his

brother abideth in death. Whosoever hateth his brother is a murderer. And ye know that no murderer hath eternal life abiding in him.

Hereby perceive we the love of God, because he laid down his life for us: and we ought to lay down our lives for the brethren.

But whoso hath this world's good, and seeth his brother hath need, and shutteth up his bowels of compassion from him, how dwelleth the love of God in him?

My little children, let us not love in word, neither in tongue; but in deed and in truth.

Uncle John closed the book. There was a long silence. My cheeks were awash with tears flowing from my touched deep places.

I dried my face on the denim-overalled knee of my Hermit Uncle John.

Dear Gletha,

I can't sleep tonight so I'm writing this under the covers with my flashlight. I feel real bad. I think ive hurt some folks something terrible. We didn't like them much so ive played a trick on them.

Well, it helps a little bit to share that simple fact with you. When do you suppose I'm going to learn to stop hurting folks. Anybody that's been hurt as bad as me should know better.

Love,

Roger

Dear Rogee,

That was the best letter I ever got from you. At least you're thinking about being careful about hurting folk.

Maybe someday you'll be able to spend your whole life reaching out to hurting folk. But I guess that's what everybody's supposed to do no matter what they spend their time at.

I'm writing this at the kitchen table by the light of the full moon which is pouring through onto the chair where you always sat. I wish you were here. I'd fix you some warm goatmilk with a touch of Karo syrup.

Love,

Gletha

BRUTUS AND THE GYPSIES

The morning after our memorable Thanksgiving with Philomel and Francis, Dad announced at breakfast that he and Mom were going into town: I was excited. The dime I'd received from Francis was burning a hole in my pocket. Finally I could get *it*.

The drugstore in town sold used books. They kept them in bushel baskets behind the Epsom salts counter. If the covers were missing, they cost a nickel. If they were in real bad shape, Shorty Partellette, the druggist, would throw in a rope of licorice. If the books were whole, he charged "one thin dime."

I'd already managed to sneak into our house copies of *Treasure Island*, Mrs. Mulock's *Barriers Burned Away* and Harold Bell Wright's *Shepherd of the Hills*. I had my heart set on Horatio Alger's *Jed, the Poorhouse Boy*. I needed to get in right away and purchase it before Quincey Emmelmann found a dime and beat me to it.

Dad torpedoed my plans: "Boy, I got a feelin' in my bones that somebody should stay here and keep an eye on things. Maybe together you and your dumb dog could at least do that much."

I knew there was no use begging to go. I fought back tears of disappointment.

Dad warned me, "You let anything happen to anything

while I'm gone, and you'll end up wishin' you hadn't."

I stood in the yard watching as they climbed into the ancient Chevy. They bounced over the frozen ruts of the dirt road leading to Pheasant Valley, disappearing behind a distant grove.

A certain peace descended on the farmstead as I watched them go. The three-legged black kitten rubbed against my leg. Skippy growled in mock ferocity and soon cat and dog were chasing each other in a wild game of widening circles.

As the circle expanded around the henyard, Brutus attacked, his honk a screaming siren of rage that his territory was being invaded. He immediately intimidated the gamesters, getting in some telling nips as he attacked.

The kitten leaped to a dangling rope and sought the solace of the haymow. Skippy found refuge behind a stack of tires in the tumble-down garage. Brutus squatted in the doorway, intent on keeping him captive as long as possible.

I picked up a heavy limb and threatened the marauding gander.

"I'm g-g-gonna k-kill you one w-w-way or t'other, you old d-d-devil goose."

He retreated to the henhouse in sullen glory.

Since it was Saturday and they would be gone much of the day, I planned to revel in forbidden activities. I would read until early afternoon.

Then, since the radio batteries had just been charged, I would sneak a listen to the Metropolitan Opera. Within my father's value system that was the ultimate act of disobedience. If he caught me escaping into the tapestry of sound, a beating would ensue, darkness or not. He always said, "I don't want no kid of mine ruined by that highfalutin' stuff."

Just as I reached the house, I heard a sound which made cold chills run down my spine. The tinkle of silver bells blew toward me on the north wind. I half expected Tinker Bell from *Peter Pan* to wave to me from my spider-encrusted attic window. The magic music was accompanied by a counterpoint of creaking wagon wheels. The sound could mean only one thing: Gypsies!

I'd heard that combination of bells and wheels only one other time. Two summers before, gypsies had set up an encampment in our far pasture on the way to Gletha's farm. They ate and sang and danced. Flute and guitar notes filtered through the moonlight. The smells from their cooking pots made maps of the world whirl through the eye of the mind.

I wished they could stay forever. However, my daddy called the sheriff and had them "cleared out a'fore mornin'." I was awakened from a deep sleep by the sound of departing wheels.

You see, one should keep a great deal of distance between oneself and gypsies. According to neighborhood wisdom they were the dirtiest people in the whole world. If gypsies were anywhere near, you'd better bolt everything down or they'd steal you blind.

Last September Isabella McClarrity, who took care of the post office in Adamsville four miles away from Pheasant Hollow, had told Hetta Bollinger, who waited tables at the Dew Drop Inn, about the family who lived away out in the middle of nowhere. "Them gypsies" had passed through just the other day and had stolen their week-old baby. The folks had gone mad with grief and nobody had been able to locate either the gypsies or the baby.

Dad's caution about making sure nothing happened to anything came crashing down on me. In my mind's eye a fearsome scenario played itself out. Swarthy men on black horses would swoop into the pasture and drive off the cows and sheep and Dad's prize plowhorses, Buster and Judy.

A line of beautiful women with coal black hair pulled back and held in place with pearl clips, dressed in snow-white blouses and blood-red skirts, danced toward the house in single file playing tambourines. They entered. A moment later they emerged carrying all of the 1847 Rogers Bros. silver plate.

I sighed. It would take years to accumulate enough Betty

Crocker coupons to replace it.

As the sounds grew louder, I simply did not know what to do. Should I run and hide with the three-legged black kitten in the haymow? Perhaps I should go out and stand in the center of the road and let them steal *me*. Then I would no longer have to endure the endless beatings.

If they concentrated on stealing me, they'd leave everything else intact so that if I ever saw my dad in the future I could avoid at least one beating.

The sounds were getting more and more distinct. My courage was lessening. I dashed to the house and coaxed Skippy inside so that he wouldn't cause a ruckus by nipping at the horses' hooves and getting kicked.

The feeling grew within me that I wanted to see without being seen. I hightailed it for the barn, climbed an interior wooden ladder and surveyed the scene through the alfalfa dusted window, the three-legged kitten cuddled in my arms.

A great white caravan rounded the bend in the road just north of our boundary line. It was pulled by a team of two high-stepping black horses. As they tossed their proud heads, the silver bridle bells pealed out primal syncopation.

The seat above the horses was occupied by a man and a woman, heavily cloaked to resist the moderate cold of an unusually mild November. I looked extra hard to try and spot any suspicious babies, but to no avail.

They slowed their pace as they came opposite our driveway. The man stood up and surveyed the scene. Seeing no one, he directed the horses to pull the caravan to the farmstead side of the road where it stopped.

He and the woman conversed. She broke into peals of laughter. He rose and stepped into the caravan through the folds of canvas. A few moments later he emerged carrying a fishing rod and reel and a gunny sack.

I thought this was the strangest sight I'd ever seen. Didn't he know that the nearest water was Lake Sumach three miles away? Sometimes my dad took out his rod and reel and made a few practice casts across the bare lawn. This seemed to me to be a strange place for the gypsy man to practice his casting.

He sat down on the seat and appeared to be baiting the hook. Rising, he took careful aim and cast whatever it was on the hook right into the center of our henyard.

The hens and roosters flew frightened away from the arrival of the foreign object. Then, some of the braver began to circle closer and closer with cautious curiosity and much clucking.

Their caution was exploded by the whooshing arrival of Brutus who with much harsh honking and wing flapping drove off all the other birds to a safe distance while he claimed the trophy. He danced coyly around whatever it was. Then, with dramatic gusto, he gobbled it down.

At the same moment, the gypsy man snapped the end of his rod to "set the hook" as I'd seen my dad and my Uncle John do so many times. The gander gave a strangled cry. The gypsy man began reeling the desperate bird inexorably across the henyard toward the fence.

The couple leaped to the ground. Keeping the line taut and the bird moving, they arrived at the fence at the same time as Brutus. The man reached over and grabbed the great bird by the long neck. He balanced the end of his rod on the ground, got his other hand around the neck and heaved the heavy bird over the fence and aimed him expertly at the top of the sack held open by the woman. They stuffed him in.

The man took out his knife and cut the end of the line right by Brutus' beak. He cut off another short piece and used it to tie shut the top of the bag. In a few short moments Brutus was bound in burlap.

Together they heaved him up on the seat. Together they climbed up and carried him inside the caravan. Together they returned. They drove off to the south. I quickly climbed out of the haymow and headed for the road. I watched them until they disappeared in the distance.

Then it hit me: the entire farmstead had been liberated!

Liberated by gypsies! I dashed to the house and freed Skippy. The kitten appeared and invited Skippy to a mad game. Their widening circles of delight were unscathed.

I got into my wagon and rode down the hill toward the barn seven glorious times without my bottom being sullied by hisses and angry jaws.

A celebratory hoop was stopped in my throat by the sound of an approaching auto. It was my folks. At that moment the enormity of the situation struck me. I'd been left in charge to see that nothing happened to anything, and now Brutus was gone!

Waves of nausea-tinged fear swept over me. Should I dash up to Dad and tell him the entire story? Such episodes of truth had led to intense suffering in the past. Maybe it would be a long time before he missed his friend. Beyond bald-faced truth, I had no choice but to wing it.

I solicitously helped carry groceries from the car without being asked. My dad looked at me strangely. "Did something happen while we were gone?" he asked suspiciously.

"N-N-No. Things w-w-were real quiet."

"What did you do?"

"I-I-I did m-m-my arithmetic homework f-f-for school Monday."

"Well, I've got a message for you from Quincey Emmelmann. He said to tell you he sure was going to enjoy *Jed, the Poorhouse Boy* which he'd bought that very minute with a dime he found on the sidewalk outside the Dew Drop Inn. I don't know what that's all about, but I've told you."

I turned from him to mask my disappointment.

He continued, "Bring your wagon over here. I'll put this bag of chickenfeed on it. You can pull it to the feed room behind the henhouse. I'll come by and unload it."

My heart sank. I knew I was lost. Every time Dad set foot in the yard, Brutus was right there.

I hauled the feed to its proper place. Dad came in and hoisted it onto its platform. He turned and took a handful of shelled corn from an open sack. I knew it was for Brutus.

I pretended to tie my shoe as he stepped into the midst of hens, roosters and guinea fowl. There were no welcoming honks. He called his name a few times. Nothing.

Fear welled up in me. I knew I couldn't keep from letting my nervousness show. Then I heard my father's voice: "Boy, get your butt out here."

I stood facing my dad.

He queried, "Do you have any idea where Brutus might be? He never leaves the yard."

"The w-w-weasel could have snuck in while I was d-d-doin' my arithmetic."

"Brutus could outfight a dozen weasels. Boy, will you stop fidgeting so we can get to the bottom of this. You got anymore good ideas?"

I fought for good ideas. "Th-Th-There's been some geese over on Specter Slough. It just m-might be that h-h-he decided not to be a t-t-tame goose anymore."

By this time I was rocking back and forth heel to toe.

Dad yelled, "Will you please stay quiet while I talk to you. Now, you appear to be real bothered by something, and I'd wager it has to do with Brutus. I know you've always hated him and wanted to eat him for Thanksgiving until we found ourselves a little substitute offering. Now, I'll give you the benefit of the doubt, and we'll just walk over to the slough and check it out."

We crossed the fields in silence. The afternoon was waning fast. We walked around Specter Slough. Strangely, there was not a single goose to be seen.

My dad was silent for a long moment. Then he said, "I don't understand it. I just don't understand. He hasn't gone from our place for weeks. That was a sure sign he liked us."

There were tears on his cheeks. He grabbed me by the shoulders and looked into my eyes.

"I think you're hidin' something. You're diddlin' up and down like a drunken cockroach. Now, I want the truth from you. WHAT. . .HAPPENED. . .to BRUTUS?"

A procession of "I should have's" flashed through my mind: I should have walked out from my hiding place and confronted the passing strangers. I should have raced to the henyard and scattered its inhabitants, risking the wing beating and pecking of the angry goose. At the point of his capture I should have bravely stepped up to the gypsies and offered myself in place of the captive bird, especially since my dad preferred him to me. In the light of my father's state of mind at the moment I should have told the truth back in the farmyard.

I finally managed to stammer out, "Th-The gy-gy-gypsies st-stole him."

The force of the blow caught me off guard. I found myself sprawled face downward in the frozen mud, flecked with the droppings of the wild geese who grazed on the shoreline grasses.

My body automatically curled into the fetal position with my arms around my head.

My daddy leaned over me, and in a low voice laced with quiet venom he grated out, "I've always regretted the day we took you out of that orphanage. I forgot to tell them one thing. I forget to tell them I didn't want no liar. You know there's one thing in the world I can't stand, and that's a liar. Brutus wasn't stolen by no gypsies. There ain't no gypsies in this part of the country durin' cold weather. They're all in Floryda stealin' oranges."

He punctuated his words with sharp kicks to my butt. I was grateful for my heavy sheepskin coat which armored me from any real injury beyond the terrible humiliation. There was no armor for that.

His final words were, "Now don't you move from there until you decide to tell me what really happened, you dirty, good-for-nothing little liar. When you've made your decision, you can come back to the house and not before. I'll be waitin' for you in my rockin' chair by the stove."

The last words trailed off into a whisper. I knew he was

moving into another of his darknesses. The rocking chair was the throne of his utter despair from which he ruled us all.

He gave me a final hard kick in the ribs which left me breathless. I lay there without moving, listening to the slow dull scrunch of his departing footsteps.

I burst into tears as I ticked off in my mind my list of losses: the loss of my dad's surprising laughter over the past two days; the loss of *Jed, the Poorhouse Boy*; the loss of Francis and Philomel; and yes, even the loss of the brutal Brutus.

I moved only enough to unbutton the top two buttons of my coat, unsnap the huge pocket on the front of my bib overalls and remove my constant companion, the small yellow teddy bear. I wiped my tears again and again on the increasingly worn spot between his ears.

In the distance I heard the mysterious tones of an owl's hoot. In my heart's eye I imagined a huge, soft-feathered bird descending, taking me gently in its talons and carrying me off to a land where gypsies included me in their eternal dance under the full moon.

I wished that Gletha, the goatlady, might suddenly appear at my side, descending majestically from the north on the November wind, her soft cloths flying. She would enfold me and magically deliver me back to her shack. She'd give me warm goat milk sweetened with Karo syrup. I could live happily ever after.

Instead, I took the only course open to me. I rose slowly from the ground and prepared to seek refuge with my Hermit Uncle John. As I placed the bear back in its pocket, I felt the frozen film of tears between his ears.

Numb inside, I walked in a daze across the fields. As I neared the holy lake, I became aware of being embraced by something beyond myself. It was different from the voices of my Uncle John's "friends" on the rock.

I was invaded by a healing dancing sound. I'd heard it once before. An orchestra on the radio had played something called the "Hungarian Rhapsody." Now, a single violin moved through a counterpoint of strident, dainty, earthy patterns. My feet wanted to dance while my ravaged body relaxed into a deep peace.

The music seemed to carry with it a rare incense which engulfed all my senses. It felt as if I wasn't simply approaching my Hermit Uncle's cabin. I was entering a magic land of mystery deeper and more complex than the red fire and the voices.

I heard the cadence of paws on the entry path. I knew that Tiny was rushing to greet me. Why wasn't she barking her usual warning that signaled my approach?

She burst out to the field edge and stopped abruptly almost under my feet. I caught an overhanging branch to break my stumbling fall.

I saw immediately why she had not barked. She bore in her mouth a priceless trophy: the severed head of Brutus the gander.

I paused in absolute amazement. Though I had witnessed his capture, I had somehow not anticipated his immediate death. I felt a strange pang of loss. I had no other center on which to fling some of the anger related to my father's brutality.

The folded-in figure of my uncle appeared in the gathering dusk. His step was lighter, as if inspired by the enfolding music.

He hugged me warmly. Then he lead me by the hand toward a far clearing where his small barn stood. He spoke excitedly. "You've g-got to m-m-meet some special f-f-friends of m-m-mine. I d-didn't expect them anymore this y-y-year. But they a-a-arrived this afternoon. They always m-make me so h-h-happy."

The music grew more intense as we neared its source. We stepped into the clearing. I gasped. There stood the gypsy caravan. The black horses grazed nearby, the breeze sounding through their bridle bells.

Framed before the barn's open door was a great fire.

Illumined by the flames was the man who had "fished" so successfully that afternoon. He was playing the violin.

At one side of the blaze sat the beautiful woman. She was gazing contentedly into the fire. With one hand she turned the handle of a makeshift spit. On the spit was mounted the now-gleaming, browning carcass of the great roasting goose.

The man saw us coming. He brought his musical phrase to a close and laid his violin on the seat of the caravan. There was a long moment of silence broken only by the sound of Tiny's teeth crunching through the goose head.

My Uncle John drew me forward and held out my hand to the approaching stranger. In his excitement his stammer deepened. "B-B-Bruno, this is my n-n-nephew, R-R-Roger. Roger, this is m-m-my f-f-friend, B-B-Bruno."

Bruno took my hand and said in faintly accented English, "I'm glad my music flowed over the fields, inviting you to our feast."

The woman, startled from her reverie when the music stopped, rose and left her task for a moment to step across the yard toward us. Outlined against the fire, her blossoming belly revealed that she was very pregnant. Wordlessly, she folded her hands around Bruno's and mine which were still joined.

Uncle John said, "And th-th-this is Martitia."

She dazzled me with a smile and returned to turning the spit.

Bruno asked, "Do you live around here?"

I described the farmyard in detail. His eyes flicked to the roasting goose.

He turned to me and commented, "I think we drove by your house this afternoon."

"No," I responded. "You *st-st-stopped* by our house."

"You were there?"

"I w-w-was hiding in the hayloft. I saw you c-c-catch old B-B-Brutus."

Uncle John intervened. "D-D-Did any of this h-h-have anything to do with your d-dad beating you and you c-c-coming over here?"

"It had everyth-th-thing to do w-w-with it!"

In one long run on sentence, scarcely pausing for breath, I poured out the whole story about my dad and Brutus. I let them know that the beating was specifically caused by his disbelief in my tale of the gypsy theft.

Bruno's face darkened. In the waning light I thought I saw tears in his eyes. He knelt down and folded me in his arms, saying, "My father beat me also. He said all boys need to be beaten. It makes them tough.

"It was a terrible life. I came to hate him. If my child is a son I will never beat him to make him tough. I will stroke his back to make him gentle."

As he spoke he stroked my back. It felt wonderful.

My Uncle John interrupted the scene with a sharp word: "I th-th-think m-m-maybe we menfolk m-might oughta' take a little stroll up t-to Shaman's Point b-b-before supper."

He stared hard at Bruno. Bruno looked profoundly uncomfortable as he turned and spoke briefly to Martitia.

Uncle John started toward the great granite outcropping. Tiny, face flecked with gander blood, quickly took the lead. Bruno and I followed silently behind.

Partway up the path Bruno suddenly stopped. As he spun around, his hand dropped to a knife in a sheath on his belt which I noticed now for the first time. He looked intently around him.

His voice was tight: "I could have sworn there was someone following us, but I don't see anyone."

"N-N-Neither do I," I returned. I thought I heard a low chuckle from an unseen presence, but it could have been the wind in the dead leaves of the black walnut trees below.

We emerged on the top of the rock. A red fire was glowing on the tip. Uncle John had probably lighted it to balance the chill of the November wind. Or it could have been blazing before we arrived. I was never sure.

We sat down by the fire. The sky in the west was deep crimson. To the east a vee of late-flying Canadian honkers wended their way beneath the scattered clouds. They usually flew directly over the Point and headed southwest. Tonight, however, they arced to the north as if unwilling to fly through the incense arising from their basting brother.

Uncle John motioned us to sit on fire warmed rocks. He put a firm hand on Bruno's shoulder. In the presence of his "friends" the knots disappeared from his tongue.

"Bruno, I've often talked to you about settling down and getting rid of the terrible uncertainties of wandering. But you say it's 'in your blood.' I think it's just in your head. You've got a baby coming. You can't steal your way across the country. It wouldn't be right. When you touch something that's someone else's, you violate them.

"My brother, Rog's dad, is terribly ill in his mind. By stealing the goose, one of his only friends, you've driven him over the edge into another kind of darkness. Again the boy has been fearfully beaten. When will you learn, my young friend, that whenever you touch one thing, something somewhere else quivers. The spider catches a fly on the rim of the net. The center feels the vibrations."

Bruno stared at the toes of his elegantly embossed boots. Then he looked at me and said quietly, "I'm sorry that my actions hurt you. I guess I must be more careful about shaking the web of the world."

Uncle John turned his head so that Bruno could not see his pleased, shy grin.

The gypsy continued, "I do have a gun. I could have killed squirrels or rabbits. But we tire of squirrels and rabbits. The chickens looked so fat and nice. I didn't even see the gander. When it swallowed the bait, I thought we had been gifted by God!"

It was dark now except for the red light from the fire. The moment made me painfully aware of how our insensitive joke had hurt the outcasts Philomel and Francis the night before. Below, I could see the cooking blaze with Martitia outlined against it. In the eyes of most folk, beautiful as she was, she was an outcast too. She was still stolidly turning the spit whose occupant was emitting an incense that set taste buds alive all the way to the rock tip.

Uncle John continued, "I guess I find it hard to understand how we hurt people real bad without thinkin' or knowin' when we should've thought and knowed."

He left us sitting in an extended silence to let the lessons take root. Tiny, as if sensing our discomfiture, licked our dangling hands in turn. Finally, the smell of the roasting goose overcame her. She began to dance in the direction of descent.

My Hermit Uncle John pulled himself slowly to his feet and started down the path, whispering a word of quiet benediction to his "friends." Bruno put a conspiratorial arm around me. Co-sinners, perhaps we could discover ways to keep each other from shaking the edge of the world's web too hard.

Arriving at the barn, Martitia addressed a foreign tongued word to Bruno. He announced that the gander was at a perfect point to be the center of a feast.

Uncle John disappeared into his cabin. The three of us removed the bird from the spit and nestled him into a huge wooden bread making bowl which Bruno had retrieved from the caravan. He quickly checked the horses' tethers. We processed, bearing the bird which was for Bruno both prize and sin offering.

The cabin table had been set for four. Brutus was enthroned in the central place of honor. He was surrounded by fresh baked bread, fried potatoes and honeyed rutabagas.

Hands were joined around the table. A Presence was affirmed.

Slipping the knife from his belt sheath, Bruno cut thick slices of the fragrant meat and placed them on eagerly offered plates.

Martitia warmed me with a special smile as I slowly chewed my first bite. She laughed as I broke into a beatific grin. At long last I was feasting on my enemy.

Dear Gletha,

My daddy beat me real bad again. It wasn't my fault. A friend of my Hermit Uncle John's who's a gypsy stole Dad's pet goose and I got blamed.

From what I understand from Uncle John nobody can do nothing without somebody else being touched. Is that true?

This will be very short since I'm writing it under the covers with my flashlight but I wanted to check it out.

Love,

Roger

Dear Rogee,

Aunt Jennie Mauldin just dropped by with your last letter. She says she'll wait for a reply if I make it quick, so this'll be short, like yours.

I'm glad you've got to know a man of sense. After all the time you hung around with me in the woods, you should've learned that all life is woven together. I'm sorry you got hurt again. Sometimes it takes pain to learn the truths at the heart of everything. Jenny is fidgeting.

Love,

Gletha

THE CHRISTMAS MIRACLE
AT PETER-THE-ROCK

It was nearly midnight. My Hermit Uncle John and I sat at the tip of Shaman's Point, remembering the long day which had passed. I always liked the Fourth of July better than Christmas. The summer garden (which he laboriously watered, one pail at a time) and the ice in the icehouse combined to enable a feast fit for all the ancient sages whose spirits hovered by the holy lake.

My stomach rumbled contentedly as it recalled homemade ice cream sampled directly from the paddle as I finished the turning task. This was followed by a delightful meal centered on fried chicken (with a taste of ice cream to check out just how it was "setting up" in the freezer). The chicken was surrounded by fresh green beans and bits of crisp fried bacon, boiled red potatoes and wilted lettuce salad (followed by another foray into the freezer to discover that the ice cream had indeed frozen to a perfect consistency).

My daddy was in a darkness. The sacramental time around the table had completely erased the images of terror wrecked upon my back and heart by the irrational blows of his ever present horse whip.

Following the main course, my Hermit Uncle John brought

out an incredible angel food cake. We opened the freezer yet another time. We piled an unbelievable mountain of the vanilla laced delicacy on the fragile foundation. We tempted fate by dribbling a generous amount of wild strawberry preserves and grated black walnuts over the ensuing mountain. There was no collapse.

The only collapse occurred when we finished the feast and lay sated in the shade beneath the great oak tree in the nap haunted, bee buzzing afternoon. All summer long the sun had focused on the countryside with peculiar intensity. Lake Sumach was at its lowest in years. The worst drought in memory had the land in its grip. There had been some question as to whether or not fireworks should be exploded. It was decided that they must be more carefully aimed out over the lake itself.

And now we sat at the tip of Shaman's Point. The smoke from the fireworks drifted lazily over the moonlit lake. The finale had been spectacular. An American flag flared from a frame by the boat docks at Kahler's Korner while rockets glared redly—and greenly and bluely. Everyone watching from their autos honked their horns. The tintinnabulation of rockets exploding, symphonic braying by Fords and Chevies, with a slight sprinkling of De Sotos and Pontiacs, and the clanging of the bell in the slender steeple of the Baptist Church of Peter-the-Rock all contributed to the fervor of patriotism in the gathered hearts.

For everyone, that is, except my Hermit Uncle John. When the ruckus peaked, he buried his head in his knees and wept. All he could think of was the rockets' red glare at the Battle of the Marne and his friends dying in his arms. It was my turn to hold *him* in *my* arms.

There was no moon. The stars bore through the lid of the sky like the points of sunlight which forced their way through the shingle cracks in our aging barn roof.

When my Uncle's sobs subsided, we sat in the firefly marred darkness and stared off into the distance. The sounds of the Six Fat Dutchmen playing for the dance at Kahler's Korner rode the faint breeze. I particularly liked their rendition of "The Clarinet Polka." Uncle John said that in the days when he used to dance that had been a real favorite. The ripples on the water seemed to capture parallel rhythms.

Suddenly, in the darkness we were blinded by light. Momentarily shocked, we couldn't identify the source. A sharp explosion tore the air. Tiny howled in fright and leaped into my arms. We watched in awe as a rocket-like object lifted from the distant fireball. Like a late-comer to the lakeside display it rose lazily into the air.

A simultaneous gasp of recognition escaped from us as we identified the falling object. It was the slender, blazing steeple of the Baptist Church of Peter-the-Rock. The church bell tolled a final time as it slid into the water, silencing itself in the holy lake.

As the church walls continued to burn, the outlines of the windows could be seen. They looked like eyes on a Halloween jack o' lantern. This obscure hall of heaven had been suddenly transformed into an inferno.

I was so dumbfounded that I began to sing, "This little light of mine, I'm gonna' let it shine; let it shine, let it shine, let it shine." The frightened dog let out a mournful howl.

We watched transfixed as the sacred building's outer shell sank gracefully inward. A cascade of sparks lifted upward, looking for all the world like one of the fountains of fire in the earlier display.

A neat, square altar of flame glowed on the great rock. I remembered the wandering evangelists who shouted in the Pheasant Valley park about offerings acceptable to God— about sin offerings and burnt offerings and calves sacrificed on altar horns by high priests.

I hoped that none of Toppy Mackin's cows were wandering in the area as they often did, leaving their "pies" which were later encountered by disgruntled Sunday worshipers. I half-expected to later hear that a Holstein carcass had been discovered by those who sifted through the results of the conflagration.

We watched as cars raced from the festivities at Kahler's Korner around the lakeshore to the church parking lot. Soon a circle of lesser lights surrounded the dying flames. Human figures were outlined against the glow. A sound crept across the waters. The folks were singing a memorial hymn to their fallen sanctuary: "The Old Rugged Cross."

The cross. I'd forgotten about that as the steeple had sunk beneath the surface. The people were real proud of their steeple cross. Paul Taver, the blacksmith, had heated iron rods white-hot and woven them into a cross which with great ceremony and considerable danger had been affixed to the beacon point ever outlined against the sky. It reminded plowmen and passersby of a Presence that transcended the petty battles that occasionally strained the little congregation to the breaking point.

My Hermit Uncle John uttered the first words since the explosion: "I w-w-wonder what'll c-c-come of all of this? It'll t-take a miracle to get those folks together enough t-t-to do whatever it is the Jesus I read about in the Bible wants them to do. S-S-Seems like they have a little trouble using the flesh God blessed through an empty tomb to live out the kind of loving that survived the cross they stuck on their st-st-steeple."

He rose to leave. Tiny, still quaking in my arms, sent a whine in his direction requesting a transfer. I handed her to Uncle John. He nestled the frightened dog on his shoulder like a needy infant. He led the way down the narrow path. Though lighted only by stars and fireflies, our feet had found their way so many times that only the inner light of familiarity was needed.

Our journey was interrupted by my Hermit Uncle John's pausing for his nightly benediction: "Good night, good friends." A wind borne response hymned in our hearts. Then all was silent.

I glanced over my shoulder where the sky had been aglow

with the dying embers of the church. It was now enhanced with the scarlet intensity of fresh fire on Shaman's Point. Perhaps the "friends" had gathered to mourn the destruction of another holy place as their own places had been so often desecrated many years ago and continued to be.

The next morning I headed over to Kahler's Korner to replenish Uncle John's supply of sugar which had been depleted by the Fourth of July feast. It seemed like most of the folk from Sunrise Township were gathered there to discuss the tragic happenings of the previous midnight. So many folk were gathered that Hank Kahler moved everybody into the dance hall and served free coffee "as a public service to those upset by the tragedy of last night."

As usual, I was completely ignored. The Six Fat Dutchmen had not taken away their equipment. I crouched down behind the bass drum to hear what I could hear.

I got lucky. Ginger MacIntyre and Felicity Evans sat down in the trumpet players' chairs right in front of me. Felicity had spent the Fourth with cousins in Hunterville. Ginger had been in on everything, including the fact that her husband, Willard, had drunk coffee with old Doc Workington at the Dew Drop Inn in Pheasant Valley earlier in the morning. About one a.m. he'd been trying to deliver Maudie Milsaps' first baby. The infant had seemed real reluctant to leave the security of its mother's womb.

Felicity and Ginger digressed slightly as they murmured mutual sympathy for the poor little tyke's being born to a daddy with only one leg, particularly if it turned out to be a boy. Billy Milsaps' limb had been blown clean off on Iwo Jima—so clean, it was affirmed, that there was nothing left to hang anything artificial on. Felicity said, "He'll just never be able to *really* play ball with his own son."

Ginger continued, "During a lull in the proceedings, nurse Cleota Collins had rushed in to tell Doc Workington that a drifter just stumbled into the hospital with some bad burns on his right arm and the right side of his face. His clothes were charred.

"Old Doc Workington left the delivery room and cleaned up the silent, suffering man the best he could. Then Maudie's screams summoned him back. When Doc and Cleota returned to check on the burn victim, he'd disappeared. A wrinkled dollar bill and three pennies had been left on the examining table (Cleota later reported that Doc had tears in his eyes as he pocketed the fee).

"But Felicity, you ain't heard nothing yet. Glenn Gunderson confessed to having a part in the terrible thing that happened last night."

Glenn was something of a ne'er-do-well who worked off and on for the county road department. You'd see him on summer days dozing on the mower seat behind Pete, his brokendown plowhorse, mowing the roadsides.

Glenn had the sorry reputation of drinking too much, slapping his wife around and being the worst liar in Sunrise Township.

His major accomplishment had been fathering three sons less than a year apart in age: George and Geoff and Giles. They terrorized the school playground and the entire township. They were ever putting me down by leading a chorus of mockers who improvised complex depictions of my terrible stammer. Glenn was real proud of his boys.

At this point, I found myself listening to three conversations whirling around me at once. I pieced together the rest of the story on my own.

When the revelers at Kahler's Korner had rushed toward the flames the night before, they found the pastor, Philotus Pfitzer, helplessly weeping over the demise of his corner of the Kingdom of God. He was soaked with sweat from standing too close to the avenging flames.

Philotus was affectionately called pastor Phil or Pastor Pfitz by everyone. Everyone that is expect Clarissa Kahler, the *grande dame* of Sunrise Township who always droned out "Rev-er-end Pfit-zer," demanding that church affairs be conducted according to her will as if she were God's personal spokesperson.

Pastor Pfitz was a skin-and-bones little man in his late fifties. He'd never quite achieved five foot in height. When in Clarissa's presence, he always seemed to shrink another four inches. When he walked, he always listed slightly to the left. A heavy black Bible was omnipresent in his left armpit.

He took the Scriptures to heart. For him every word was Gospel truth. Since Jesus had never married, neither had he. There was some kidding around the township, particularly from the Roman Catholics, about the Church of Peter-the-Rock being served by a Baptist monk.

The last person to arrive on that fateful midnight was Glenn Gunderson. He swerved his dilapidated pickup into the parking lot, causing a couple of onlookers to leap for their lives. He stumbled over to the weeping pastor and fell on his knees, his toes perilously close to the dying embers.

There was a rush of folk across the lot to hear what was transpiring. Glenn, his words slurred by celebration, gasped out, "Pastor Phil, I've got to confess and receive the forgiveness of Almighty God and his Son, Jesus Christ, our Lord, and the Holy Ghost."

Having covered all his bases in terms of sources for forgiveness, he paused for breath and then continued: "Pastor Phil, part of what happened tonight is my fault. Since I'd worked with explosives during the War in the South Pacific, the road department hired me to blast a roadbed through Garver Gap. I loaded the dynamite onto my truck. But I knew I couldn't leave it there over the holiday, and I sure couldn't take it home. My boys tend to be a little lively, and I just didn't know what they might do if they got a'hold of it (I thought that was one of the better decisions he'd made in all his troublous days)!

"I looked around for a real safe place, and the safest place I could think of was the church. I slipped in day before yesterday when there wan't anybody around and hid it in the corner of the basement behind the screen where the Christmas stuff is stored. I spread the kings' robes over it and set the manger scene on top of it so's nobody would suspect there was anything out of the ordinary even if they started lookin'."

He paused for a moment. The crowd stood in breathless silence, completely transfixed by the tale. Before Pastor Phil could respond, Glenn let out a strangled gasp: "Omigod! I just happened to think: the baby Jesus and his Ma and Pa were all blown to smithereens when the dynamite went. Omigod! Omigod! Omigod! I'll roast in hell for that for sure."

As he let forth a further mournful stream of "Omigods" the half-charred board on which his feet rested as he knelt flamed up once more. There were cries of alarm from the gathered congregation. Before anyone could come to his rescue, their cries were drowned by his scream as the sharp pain levitated him upwards.

He scrambled down the narrow path from the rocky height, where the extinct edifice had once risen, toward the lake below. There was a loud splash as he plunged into the shallows where there was a chance for both his blistered soles and his blasted soul to be soothed by the sacred waters.

As these tales swirled through the crowd in a variety of versions, another theme began to play out: probably the burned drifter had snuck into the church to spend the night. He may have fallen asleep with a lighted cigarette. The cigarette could have set the upstairs on fire. The man was awakened when his clothes caught fire. He got away as fast as he could. He was lucky in that he got away *before* Glenn Gunderson's dynamite exploded.

Toppy Mackin reflected the general feeling of the crowd: "If that there drifter hadn't got his butt out o' there real fast, he'd be orbiting the moon about now."

Pastor Phil stepped to the center of the dance floor. He was shifting from one foot to the other and listing slightly forward since he had removed the great Bible from his armpit and was extending it in front of him as if the very act would silence the high-pitched, excited voices. He tried to get the crowd's attention by clearing his throat, but to no avail.

Glenn Gunderson, seeing the discomfiture of the little man, stepped slowly forward on his parched, carpet-slippered feet and shouted in his *basso profundo* voice, "Shut up, everybody! The preacher's got something to say."

The onlookers settled into silence. Pastor Phil cleared his voice nervously, a sickly smile struggling to his lips: "All those times I've condemned this place as a den of sin, I guess I never expected to be proclaiming the Word of the Lord from it. It just goes to show, you never can tell just what the Lord will use next.

"Early this morning as I was prayin' for guidance, the Spirit came over me and led me into this plan. Tomorrow being Sunday, I want us all to gather at the wreckage of the church. God's revealed a plan to me for its rebuilding."

His voice grew more impassioned as he wound up and forgot he was standing if not in the midst of Gomorrah, at least in Sodom. "I want ev-er-y-bod-y to be there whether or not they're a baptized member of Peter-the-Rock. God has a plan and a use for ev-er-y-bod-y. We'll all come together and feel together the descent of the dove and a new Pentecost right there in the midst of the charred remains of Peter-the-Rock!"

A great cheer went up. Since the picnic tables at the edge of the woods had not burned, there was general agreement that a potluck meal could be assembled. There was *no* agreement over who should bring the potato salad and who should bring the baked beans. It was finally decided that Marjorie Kewhler and Harriet Binder should bring a pot of each. I was glad that was finally cleared up. The planet Mars would have glowed even more angrily over this domestic battleground.

I returned with my sack of sugar to my Hermit Uncle John's. I shared all the news and rumor and speculation I'd heard. He said quietly, "I'm m-m-most concerned about the poor d-d-drifter who is probably scared to death that the authorities or somebody will catch up w-w-with him."

I queried, "Uncle John, c-c-can we go over to Peter-the-Rock tomorrow morning. Th-th-they said there'd be something everybody could d-d-do. I know I'd l-like to help some. And you c-c-can do just about anything."

Uncle John dried his hands on the dishtowel he'd been using on our breakfast dishes. He wiped his cheeks on the corner of the towel. I saw that his eyes had teared up. He mused quietly, "Ever since I got back from the W-W-War the folks around here have thought I was queer. Th-Th-They shun me whenever I'm around, and they are always l-laughin' and callin' me old, d-d-d-dumb John.

"All that hurts so bad. I doubt that they'd w-w-want either one of us around while the church is g-g-gittin' built. I think we'd just better keep our d-d-distance from all those g-g-good Christian folk who make Mars weep with their goings-on."

I decided to bide my time. When the following morning arrived, I announced with all the drama I could summon that I was going to join the worshipers at Peter-the-Rock for their special time together. I hoped they would be desperate enough to include us both. I said as much to my Hermit Uncle John.

To my amazement he agreed to go if it would make me feel better and I would stop sniveling. He stepped to the kitchen and removed a fresh gooseberry pie from the cabinet, commenting, "We'd best take something for the potluck."

He pulled down one of his woven reed baskets from a hook on the kitchen wall. He wrapped the pie in a dishtowel and nestled it carefully in its soft, flexible carrier. He took from another hook his World War I field kit which contained two of everything needed to eat: knives, forks, spoons, plates and cups. He draped the carrying strap around my neck. He donned the only piece of an army uniform I ever saw him wear: a broad-brimmed khaki hat with a prominent oak leaf and acorn cluster resplendent on the side.

We walked slowly around the lake. The sun was hot. We could hear cars making their way to the church parking lot. Everyone was going to want to make sure the church was rebuilt to his or her specifications.

The congregation was milling around the scene of destruction. People were flipping over hunks of charred board, hoping to find something of value. Little was found. Finally, Pastor Pfitz got everyone assembled. Uncle John and I had been there quite a few minutes. Everyone ignored us.

Pastor Pfitz cleared his throat. The crowd buzzed toward silence. He shifted the great Bible from his left armpit. He began to fumble it open. Glenn Gunderson, hoping to work his way back into the good graces of God and the preacher, limped quickly forward and said, "Let me hold that for you, Reverend."

Glenn's huge hulk holding the Word on extended hands completely obscured the tiny pastor from most of his listeners. Undeterred, he proclaimed: "I would remind you of the Word of God found in Nehemiah 2, 5:

And I said unto the king, 'If it please the king, and if thy servant have found favor in thy sight, that thou wouldest send me unto Judah, unto the city of my fathers' sepulchres, that I may build it.'

"As I stood by the dying embers last night, I felt caught up in the Spirit. I knew I had been sent unto this Judah to build."

His words were interrupted by a loud chorus of "Amen!" and scattered applause.

He paused in surprise, recaptured his line of thought and continued, "We cannot let the forces of darkness overcome us. The Devil found an instrument to attempt the working of his evil ways."

Glenn Gunderson shuffled his sore feet guiltily, nearly dropping the Bible.

Pastor Phil was on a roll. For the next half-hour we were admonished to forestall the plans of the wicked and focus on plans to rebuild the house of God. Standing on the edge of the crowd, Uncle John and I were nowhere near a picnic table. The baked offering of gooseberry pie was getting a little heavy. As our hands got tired, we passed it back and forth between us.

Finally, after extended references to the feeding of the five thousand, Pastor Phil encouraged everyone to sit down at the scattered picnic tables and talk together about just what everyone might contribute to the task before them.

There was a rush to claim the tables. Children grabbed chicken legs and fresh baked rolls and scrambled down the path to pursue minnows in the shallows. Uncle John and I moved hesitantly through the rush. We felt invisible. We wanted to do something that would make it obvious that we wanted to be a part of what the church folk were hoping to do. There was no offer of a place at any table.

My Hermit Uncle John had that same look on his face as when he'd come back from Kahler's Korner after having been called "old, dumb John." He whispered to me, "These folk may know about Nehemiah, but they don't know much about Jesus."

I said, "They just don't know what they're m-m-missing. Some table could have the best gooseberry pie in Sunrise Township."

He replied, "I th-th-think maybe we better find us a place beneath an oak tree in the grove. We'll just share the pie by ourselves."

We walked across the parking lot to a lone table-shaped flat rock about a foot high which was nestled back in the woods away from the general jollity of the gathered congregation. A car was parked near the path to the rock. We discovered that the rock too was occupied.

There, seated on a blanket was Billy Milsaps with Maudie and their three-day-old baby. The baby was nursing. I turned away quickly. That was the first time I'd seen an infant at a woman's breast. I was strangely embarrassed. However, I had seen something that didn't embarrass me one bit: an enormous platter of fried chicken surrounded by new peas and red potatoes. There was a pitcher of grape Kool-Aid. Billy was dishing up two plates.

Hermit Uncle John ducked his head and muttered, "W-W-We're t-t-terrible sorry. W-W-We d-didn't know a-a-anyone was h-h-here. C'mon, R-R-Rog. We'll f-f-find ourselves another p-p-place."

Maudie's insistent voice stopped us. "Wait a moment, John, I know who you are. You and the boy can stay. We got plenty. Or were you gonna' join the folk at the church picnic?"

He answered, "N-N-No. We was j-just gonna' find ourselves a q-q-quiet spot t-t-to eat a l-little p-p-pie."

Billy joined her invitation. "I've been doin' the cookin' since before Marty—that's our baby—was born. Maudie says I always make enough food for an army. I'll make you a deal. I heard you say you had some pie. I didn't get nothin' sweet baked. We'd be glad to trade chicken and vegetables for a piece of pie."

Uncle John saw me staring at the beautiful plate of golden chicken. He grinned and responded, "I reckon we j-j-just might do that. We thought w-w-we might join the f-folk at the lakeside, b-b-but we sort of f-f-felt unwelcome."

The smile left Billy's face. "We thought we might join them for a while too. Maudie was feeling real good this morning so soon after Marty's birth. She thought we might enjoy a little time in the sun. As we drove out from Pheasant Valley, I just got more uncomfortable. Ever time I'm with them people, they make me feel like a freak. All they can do is stare at where my leg was. You'd think the mine had blasted me into being some kind of a monster."

As he spoke, I removed the field kit and laid out the utensils. He did exactly as I hoped. Billy automatically heaped our plates as he continued.

"There's lots of things I can do." A look of incredible tenderness crossed his face. "I fathered myself a beautiful baby boy." Maudie blushed and held the child more closely.

"I make us a good living keeping books at the grain elevator."

As he shoved the plates across the blanket toward us, he added, "And I think I'm a real good cook when I gotta' be."

All three of us nodded in agreement.

My Uncle John said, "The folk a-a-around here h-h-have a lot of trouble w-with those of us who are d-d-different. I-I-Iffen' we don't l-look just like them, it m-m-means that we can't d-d-do nothin'."

Billy looked thoughtful for a moment and then spoke softly. "I guess maybe we make them afraid. They're afraid something terrible's gonna' happen to them the way it happened to us. If we're out of sight, they won't have to face up to that possibility. By the way, who's the young man you got with you?"

"This here's R-R-Rog. He's m-m-my brother's boy. H-H-He's with me a lot." Neither Billy nor Maudie asked any questions. I was glad.

Uncle John went on talking more freely than I'd ever heard him talk to strangers. "I was surprised that y-y-you a-a-asked us to j-join you. I know what they s-s-say about m-m-me. A boy ran b-b-by me the other day when I was at K-K-Kahler's K-K-Korner and shouted t-t-to another kid, 'Don't you l-look at old H-H-Hermit J-J-John. You'll g-get w-w-warts on your eyeballs.'"

Uncle John's eyes were filled with tears. Maudie put a comforting hand on his knee. "It's all right, John. We understand. There's been plenty a'times when Billy's come home cryin' and shoutin' and swearin' when he's heard some of the terrible things folk say. The bartender at the Dew Drop Inn started it all when we was there. We were seated at a table by the entrance to the lounge when Tred Mifflin shouted down the bar, 'Hey! Did you see old Billy Crutch Hopper out there in the family section. I wonder when he's gonna' be man enough to come in here?' We left the table right away without even finishing the lemon meringue pie. You *know* Billy is mad when he doesn't finish pie!"

Billy looked as if he'd like to "shush" his wife. My Hermit

Uncle John looked at our plates. They were all empty—Billy's and mine for the third time. He said, "W-W-Well, I g-g-guess s-s-since we're in a s-s-safe place where n-n-nobody's gonna' b-bother us, we m-m-might just finish off some p-p-pie."

He reached for the intricately woven soft reed basket. He lifted out the pie as if it were the sacred Host. Maudie stroked the side of the basket and asked, "Where did you get this beautiful thing?"

I spoke up for the first time with great pride. "He w-w-wove it himself. He m-makes all k-k-kinds of beautiful things."

Billy spoke in awestruck tones: "Well, that pie is certainly one beautiful thing."

While my Uncle John divided the pie, Maudie removed the baby from her breast. I'd long since gotten over my embarrassment. She said, "We're still not used to havin' a baby with us. We put together our picnic at the last minute and didn't even bring anything to lay the baby down in."

Then she looked at the reed basket. Her face lighted up. "John, it looks to me like Marty would just fit in your beautiful basket. Can I try?"

My Hermit Uncle John exploded with a rare laugh, "S-S-Sure. I n-n-never thought I'd s-s-see one of m-my baskets used as a c-c-cradle!"

Maudie lined the basket with the dishtowel which had been around the pie. She wrapped the baby in a tiny log cabin patterned quilt which she proudly said she'd sewed herself. She laid him tenderly in the basket. He looked for all the world like I imagine Moses must have looked when they put him in the bulrushes.

With incredible grace, Billy rose to a standing position on his single leg. He stood for a moment balanced like a circus tightrope walker. He reached up and steadied himself on the heavy branch of the sheltering oak tree just above us. He reached down and picked up the basket by its long looped handle.

He hung it on the branch. The summer breezes rocked it gently. The baby slept.

Lowering himself to the ground he tore into the pie. We all followed suit. The savory delicacy was indeed sacramental.

We settled back for a final glass of Kool-Aid. Maudie queried shyly, "John, my ma told me a story about you and her. Would you like to hear it?" She flashed him a smile that was irresistible.

He shifted uneasily and grinned. "I-I-I think your p-p-prob'ly gonna' tell it whether I-I-I want to hear it or not."

"Well," Maudie said in a tone that suggested a revelation from the halls of the gods themselves, "my ma told me that you were just about the handsomest man in Sunrise Township before the Great War. She said that she was just crazy about you—and that you used to pay her a bit of attention at the barn dances. Then just as it looked like things might progress between you, off you went into the army and on to France.

"My ma said she used to write you letters, and you even wrote back a couple of times. She said that she really could hardly wait for you to return from the Front.

"Then when you come back, you moved away from people and wouldn't talk to her or anybody else anymore. And you moved out into that old shack in the woods, and nobody much saw you anymore.

"She finally gave up and married my pa. He was a real good man and provided for us real good. But he was real, real serious, and Ma said there was always laughter when you were around.

"It seems real strange to be sittin' here talkin' to somebody who could've been my father. You know, Pa was killed by lightnin' workin' on the railroad out of St. Cloud. He didn't even get to see his first grandchild. Ma's awful lonely now. Maybe you two oughta' say 'hello' again someday."

My Hermit Uncle John was silent. Then he whispered, "I m-m-might try t-to s-s-say 'hello.' B-B-But I'd st-st-stammer s-s-so b-bad I'd n-n-never get i-i-it out."

From the picnic grounds below a chorus of voices wafted up to us, singing, "Build, build for the glory; build for the glory of God." It was one of those endless simplistic ditties for which other words could replace build: love, sow, spin, reap, pray etc.

My Uncle John looked at the setting sun. "We'd best be gettin' back around the l-l-lake. I think w-w-we'll j-just walk through the c-c-crowd and see if any of th-th-them notices somebodies n-n-new with hands to help.

"I d-d-do want to thank you r-r-real much for includin' us."

Billy rose to his foot, this time bringing up his crutches with him. "It's been real good to be with you. Let's get the boy out of the basket so's you can take it home."

My Uncle John reached out a finger and gently stroked the cheek of the sleeping child still swaying in the caressing breeze from off the holy lake. "Keep the b-b-basket. He's r-r-ridin' on the b-breath o' God right n-n-now. I c-c-can always weave another b-b-basket."

Billy said, "Why, Maudie and me's terrible grateful. I hope we can see you again sometimes. I think us shunned folk with handicaps ought to stick together."

My Hermit Uncle John quickly responded, "*Us* handi-capped f-f-folk? If you l-l-look into their h-h-hearts, you've just described the whole human r-r-race."

He picked up the empty pie pan. I put the field kit around my neck, murmured my thanks, and together we returned to the crowd by the lakeside.

The crowd had been divided up into work teams, each with a particular responsibility for construction. At the moment there seemed to be an argument raging about the cross. The old cross, separated from the burned steeple, could be seen outlined beneath the water. There were those who wanted to bring it up and those who didn't. There were those who, if it were brought up, wanted it returned to the steeple.

However, there were those practical folk who felt it would

be much too expensive to add a steeple right away. They were countered by those who felt that God just couldn't be worshiped in a building without a steeple.

On the other hand, there were those who felt that if the cross was brought up it should be placed on the front wall to remind them of the fact that God was not mocked by the forces of the Devil and the church had risen again.

Pastor Phil was standing helplessly in the middle of the warring factions. To my surprise my Hermit Uncle John walked over to him. I followed close behind. He addressed the addled minister: "Y-Y-You don't know me v-very w-w-well. I l-live directly across the l-l-lake under Shaman's P-P-Point. I'd be g-glad to d-d-do anything I c-c-can to help. And s-s-so would the b-b-boy."

Pastor Phil seemed to be relieved at being distracted from his warring flock. He smiled for a moment. Then the smile faded. He said stiffly, "You're the hermit that worships Indian spirits—at least that's what I've heard tell. However, I'm not one to pay attention to gossip. All I need to know is if you've been baptized and born again."

Uncle John stared at him in amazement without answering. Pastor Pfitz said, "Well, are you dumb, man? If I remember right, you did ask me a question earlier. Well, answer my question now. We're not about to have unforgiven sinners working on this building. We're not going to take any chances of something like what happened happening again. Are you saved? Have you been washed in the blood of the Lamb?"

The interrogation was interrupted by a shout from the edge of the rock directly over the lake. It seems that a cadre of those in favor of raising the cross had gathered there. They were being accosted by some of those who said it couldn't be done. Wally Mertwuller said, "By God, I can do it single-handed."

Clem Finstander, the leader of the anti-cross-raisers shot back that if he did it, by God, he wasn't doing it single-handed. Wally Mertwuller asked him if he wanted to fight about it. They leaped at each other, but friends from both factions pulled them apart.

Wally turned toward the lake. Before anyone realized just what was happening, Wally kicked off his shoes, stripped the shirt off his huge frame and made a motion as if to loosen his belt. Ladies who were scraping leftover baked beans into a single pot screamed. He leered in their direction and shouted, "I'm going for it."

He turned and dove off the rock. It was later affirmed that he had snuck an unknown quantity of home-brew into the family picnic basket and had consumed it all himself.

As he dove, the closest men tumbled down the narrow path which Glenn Gunderson had traversed two nights before. There was a tremendous splash and then silence.

He had forgotten about the shallowness of the lake due to the drought. His head struck the sunken cross.

Shouts were heard from below along with the sounds of men wading into the shallows: "Get him turned over." "That's it. Ease him into shore." "Flop him over and git him drained out." "Omigod! Look at the blood pouring out of his forehead."

The final comment elicited a general rush to the edge of the rock to see the carnage below. A large group of men had now assembled. They were hoisting the unconscious Wally to their shoulders and laboriously moving up the path.

They laid him gently on the ground. Graciella Greardon who was sweet on Wally rushed forward with ice from someone's ice cream freezer. The blood was flowing from a gash generally acclaimed to have come from his encounter with the sunken cross. Graciella covered the wound with the ice which had been generously laced with rock salt.

Wally awoke with a scream. He sat up so fast that the gentle Graciella was sent sprawling in a most unladylike fashion. Wally shouted out that he'd had a vision. The crowd fell silent. Graciella regained her composure and pressed more ice to the wound while Wally witnessed.

He told the awed congregation that he'd seen himself in

hell, burning in the lake of fire, and that he'd never drink another drop and that he still felt the flame right in the middle of his forehead. He slapped away the hand that held the salt laced ice. Maddie Canton, who'd had some nurses' training, rushed up with a clean cold compress, wiped away the dirt and salt and halted the bleeding until they could get Doc Workington to put in a few stitches.

Uncle John and I stole away. We walked in silence around the lake. The evening star, the red planet Mars, named for the god of war, twinkled cynically over the distant churchly contention.

To our amazement the structure rose once again toward the heavens as the weeks of summer passed. The warring factions were still contending, according to the conversations in Kahler's Korner. Those for and against the cross had reached a truce. There would be no cross of any kind for the time being.

The word was that the church would be ready for use the first time on Christmas Eve. I gave all of this late-breaking news to my Hermit Uncle John.

I found him one evening reading his Bible under the kerosene lamp. He looked up as I came in. He saw the mark of my father's fist on my cheek. He beckoned me to him. He pressed the cool leather of the great book against my bruised flesh.

"I've been thinkin'," he mused. "I think those folk in the Baptist Church of Peter-the-Rock really need a cross."

With the Bible in his hand and me by his side and Tiny sleeping on his feet, he scarcely stammered. He continued: "We all need to be reminded that we've been loved a whole lot. The empty cross should do that. We should remember that our flesh is holy and our neighbor's flesh is holy. The Holy Babe in the manger should remind us of that. You know, R-R-Rog, I think we're just going to plant a couple little reminders of all that for those folk on Christmas Eve."

His face was engulfed in a beatific grin.

His surprise unfolded step-by-step. First he asked me to

keep an eye out at Kahler's Korner for Billy and Maudie Milsaps. When I saw them, I was to extend an invitation to "drop by for some good pie of some sort or another."

Two days later I met them. Billy practically drooled at the prospect. A couple of weeks later, Uncle John commented mysteriously that they'd been by and that all the plans had been made. He wouldn't tell me because he wanted me to be surprised as well.

However, I did begin to sense that something was evolving when he gathered great armloads of a particular reed from Massacre Slough. He cured them in his special way and laid the reeds out down the whole length of the barn. Then he began to weave.

Fall was passing quickly. I sensed that Billy and Maudie with baby Marty stopped by to visit on occasion. I could hardly wait to experience the surprise.

I was awarded the honor of helping my Uncle John weave through cold November. My fingers were freezing, but the excitement in my heart warmed me. It soon became evident that we were weaving a gigantic cross.

It was a strange December. There was little snow, and the days were surprisingly warm. As Christmas approached, I slipped down to the lake to observe the progress on the church. The shell was complete. A large potbellied stove had been installed. Rough benches had been crafted. A tiny pulpit had been built to accommodate tiny Pastor Phitz. A tall evergreen had been installed on one side. The ladies of the church had crocheted dozens of red balls. The children had strung popcorn.

No altar table had yet emerged. It wouldn't be ready until after Christmas. The electric wires had not yet been strung from the transformer at Kahler's Korner to the church. Everybody would bring a lantern to illumine the midnight service on Christmas Eve.

I heard the final plans a week before Christmas. Clarissa Kahler was inviting everybody to the Korner Store for a party early in the evening. Then there'd be a motorcade to the church for the dedication and carol singing.

The cross was finished three days before Christmas and carefully rolled so that it could be transported in Billy Milsaps' car. My Hermit Uncle John quickly turned to another project. He wove a cradle out of reeds and hung it on a manger-like frame. I knew the plan was coming quickly to a climax.

The day before Christmas my Uncle John sent me on a strange errand. I was to walk over to the church and make sure there was still a long ladder present from the construction. I did as I was told and found one laying on its side along the back of the church. Pastor Phitz passed by the church while I was looking and told me to stop lurking around his church. I was probably up to no good.

I was angry at his suspicion, so I told him that I had read how Jesus had said, "Suffer the little children to come unto me" and that I was just coming unto. He told me to stop smarting off to an adult and leave. I did. Somehow I knew in my bones that I was soon to return.

The Milsaps arrived at 9 o'clock on Christmas Eve. We loaded the cross and the manger into their trunk. We brought a second kerosene lantern, a hammer and some nails and a three-legged milking stool. We drove off around the lake. As we passed Kahler's Korner, we could see a great crowd of people enjoying the largest Christmas party ever in Sunrise Township.

The church was dark as we drove into the parking lot. We lighted the kerosene lanterns, entered the building and started a fire in the stove. Uncle John and I went around to the back of the church and brought in the ladder.

Mounting the ladder in two locations, my Hermit Uncle John put two carefully spaced pegs in the wall. Lightweight ropes which had been tied to the arms of the cross were tossed over the pegs. Billy and I pulled on the ropes. Uncle John steadied the rising cross with one of Billy's crutches. Maudie watched admiringly from a bench by the warm stove where she was nursing Marty. I wasn't even embarrassed.

Uncle John nailed the cross in place. The ropes were removed. We returned the ladder outside. The manger was placed at the foot of the great reed cross.

Billy went out to the car and returned with a box, the three-legged milking stool and a shepherd's crook. Opening the box he took out two burlap capes and handed them to Uncle John and me. I looked at mine quizzically. Then I followed his lead and put it on over my sheepskin coat. I felt I'd become a shepherd straight off a Sunday School leaflet.

Billy donned a long, stripped robe and handed a splendid dark blue cape to Maudie. She handed the sleeping Marty to Billy and slipped into the cape. She was transformed back in time nineteen hundred years.

In the distance we heard cars coming along the washboardy road toward the church. We spoke no words. We didn't have to. Some interior sense beckoned us to the front of the church.

When the first persons entered the church, they gasped. Saying not a word, they quietly filed to the benches at the front of the church, overwhelmed by the strange visitation.

Joseph, leaning on his crutches, looked down on his sleeping son, a hand resting on his wife's shoulder. Two motionless shepherds knelt in wonder. The right hand of the older rested in the manger where the sleeping baby boy grasped his thumb.

The last to arrive was Pastor Philotus Pfitzer, accompanied by Glenn Gunderson, his worn wife and trio of terrors: George and Geoff and Giles. Pastor Phil began to sputter, but Glenn, awed for the only time in his life, put a gentle but firm hand across his pastor's mouth.

At last, Pastor Phil, carrying a lantern, stepped to the pulpit. Taking the great Bible from his armpit he began to intone, "And it came to pass in those days that there went out a decree from Caesar Augustus that all the world should be taxed...."

He could go no further. His voice choked. He laid his head

in his arms on the pulpit and sobbed as if his heart would break. Most of the congregation followed suit.

When the sins and the cares and the self-deceptions were cried out, someone started "Silent Night." As one, they rose and filed past the Nativity. They paused to shake hands with Joseph, embrace Mary, squeeze the old shepherd's shoulder, pat the young shepherd on the head and stroke the cheek of baby Jesus who, now awake, giggled in response.

When the last person had left, we wearily, happily packed up our things. Uncle John and I were dropped off at his cabin. We let Tiny out and began our climb to Shaman's Point. There seemed to be an added note of excitement in the air. When my Hermit Uncle John said, "Good night, good friends," we sensed laughter on the wind.

After what everybody called the Christmas miracle at Peter-the-Rock, there was a new spirit in the congregation, at least for a little while. And when contentions would arise, someone would inevitably begin to sing "Silent Night."

Dear Gletha,

I just had the best Christmas Eve since Todd Tolliver and Mayetta Mahan got together again in Bear Run School and he started being daddy to baby Hosea which wasn't his.

There's a church across the lake which burned and got built again. The folks are almost as unpleasant as some of those in the Lakeside Church of Jesus Risen up there where you are.

Tonight, my Hermit Uncle John and I were part of the manger scene. Everybody cried. It was some of the best crying I've ever seen. I think Jesus liked it.

Merry Christmas a little late.

Love,

Roger

Dear Rogee,

I wish you were here to tell me the whole story of what really happened on Christmas Eve. But then folks have been asking that question for two thousand years.

I'm glad you had some really good crying all around you. That should have touched them all in a real way.

Happy New Year.

Love,

Gletha

TONY GREAT TURTLE

The mid-afternoon Saturday sun bore down on Massacre Slough. Crows cawed in distant fields. Meadowlarks and bobwhites sang softer melodies.

The remainder of my throw line was carefully coiled on a flat rock. I had successfully hurled the lead sinker with its attendant signal bobber and angleworm-baited hook far out into the open water.

I was pleased with my prowess. When alone or with my Hermit Uncle John these primitive casts always went well. The line never tangled. I would loop the excess line in perfect ovals on a rock while waiting for the fish to bite. When I was with my father, everything snarled. He brutalized me with his words as I sought to untie the hideous knots in the fine cord.

I had told my mother I was going fishing. She threw up her hands in despair and said, "Roger, don't you bring home any more fish. I've canned bullheads and pickled bullheads, and we've eaten fried bullheads until I just can't stand any more."

I assured her that probably my Hermit Uncle John would appreciate some. However, when I broached the subject to him on my way to the Slough he commented quietly, "What I r-r-really need is a b-b-boy to help me carry w-w-water to the garden."

I fled through the forest as quickly as possible.

Now, the bright red fishing bobber floated lazily on the water, ducking occasionally in the light breeze. Its rhythm rocked me into daydreams far removed from my present task. I was playing clarinet in a symphony orchestra at the Paris Conservatory.

That fantasy, like most fantasies, had roots in reality. On Thursday I'd slipped into the band room where contest music was laid out for consideration by those who wanted to do solos. I knew I was too young, too inexperienced to attempt participation. However, bandmaster Sherm Savola had said we could choose a piece and try it out. He didn't put any time limit on that endeavor.

My eye was drawn to the most complex cover on the table:

G. Guilhaud
1er CONCERTINO
(Morceau de Concours)
Pour Hautbois et Piano
Transcrit Pour Clarinette en si bemol
et Piano
par
PHILIPPE PAQUOT
Prix du Conservatoire de Paris

My hand gently caressed the cover. I didn't understand most of the words. I could pick out "clarinette" and "piano." But it was the magic final line which drew me. Like my model for the correct position in which to hold an instrument in my *Smith-Yoder-Bachman* lesson book, this piece was connected to the Paris Conservatory.

Feeling that I should probably wash my hands first but too fully drawn by the impulse of the moment, I lifted the sheet music carefully from the table as from an altar. I opened it. The notes were much smaller than those in my beginner and intermediate books. They cascaded across the page like tiny black water bugs in a still pool. There were strange words underneath them like *tenuto* and *a tempo* and *cantabile*.

I knew I was standing on the frontier of a long imagined land with its own language far beyond my father's whip and Sunrise Township. I slipped the magic sheets into my bookbag. That night I placed the treasure beneath my pillow. Finally, I had something concrete to dream upon. All that night I bowed to full houses of applauding listeners as I soloed with the Paris Conservatory orchestra.

My reverie was broken by the gentle swish of my throw line spinning off the rock with nary a knot. I glanced at the glistening water as I grabbed for the line. The bobber was nowhere to be seen. I jerked the line to set the hook in the mouth of the fish. I began to retrieve the struggling captive, carefully recoiling the line on the rock.

As the fish came close to shore it became evident that I had hooked a prize indeed. The herculean splashing excited me. I stepped to the shore and carefully drew out the biggest, fattest bullhead I'd ever seen. I was sorry my daddy was not here. For once he could have been proud of me on a lakeshore.

Suddenly the fish stopped its desperate flopping. I was surprised since I could clearly see that it had not swallowed the hook which was firmly anchored in its jaw.

Looking out across the slough, I knew from the perfect reflection of the reeds in the glassy water that the breeze had stilled. I was overwhelmed by absolute silence. The sky was clear of marauding crows. Meadowlarks and bobwhites were mute.

An eerie feeling crept over me. I sensed another's presence. I turned, and there, not ten feet from me, leaning against a lightning-blasted oak, was an old man. A broad-brimmed leather hat shadowed his face.

I nearly jumped out of my skin. Then, as our eyes met, a strange kind of peace settled over me while fear stood waiting in the wings. Bravado prompted me to overcome my discomfort by bragging to the stranger.

"Hi. I'll bet you've never seen a bullhead this big and fat!"

Amazement stopped my flow of words. I'd just spoken a sentence with three "b's" and an "f" and I hadn't stammered!

I decided to push my luck and continued, "Just a minute. I'll put my fish on my stringer. There's five more a lot smaller than him which I caught earlier."

Rejoicing in the clarity of my speech, I stepped down to the edge of the slough. The fish on my stringer were all alive. They seemed poised expectantly in the water, all facing the shore. I added the great fish. It did not thrash in the water but floated in suspended waiting.

I walked toward the old man. His face was expressionless. I said, "My name is Rog. Are you from around here? I ain't never seen you before, have I?"

The absolute silence of stranger and nature continued. Uncomfortable with quiet, I ran out a stream of words which came quickly, glibly off my tongue.

"Do you know where you are? This here's Massacre Slough. It's really more a lake than a slough though it's more slough over there to the east where the muskrat mounds are. Best bullhead fishing in the county. They're fatter here than anywhere else. Say, would you like to know just why the fish are so fat?"

The stranger remained silent. I could not.

I continued, "My daddy told me all about it the last time we was here. My daddy doesn't talk to me much without yelling, but I guess because I got my line untangled he could tell me something useful as a kind of reward.

"It's all the fault of them damned Sioux Indians. That's what he always calls them. He's always told me that the only good Indian is a dead Indian. Now his brother, my Hermit Uncle John, feels just the opposite, but my daddy thinks he's real crazy.

"You see, their granddaddy and a whole bunch of other settlers was killed by them damned Sioux Indians. Their bleeding bodies were dumped into this very slough. My daddy says that because of all that blood everything fish eat grows real good and that's why anything that swims in these waters is extra fat.

"Them Indians got their comeuppance though. A whole bunch were caught and taken to Fort Snelling and hanged. Now, what do you think of that?"

The stranger only looked at me more intently. In the unaccustomed flow of words I had not noticed the darkening sky. The possibility of a continued monologue was cut off by a sharp flash of lightning over the slough and a horrendous crash of thunder.

I flinched and continued with one last bit of wisdom: "My daddy says if you get caught in the woods in a storm you better head for an open place because trees draw lightnin', just like that one you're leanin' against. Why don't you follow me?"

I lit out for a nearby field. Reaching my destination, I turned around and saw I hadn't been followed. The storm passed as quickly as it came. Only a few drops of rain had fallen.

I ran back to the lakeshore. The stranger had disappeared. The crows were quarreling again in the distance.

To cover my discomfiture at the man's unexpected exit, I said aloud, "W-W-Well, I g-g-guess I'd b-better take my fish up t-t-to Uncle John. I sure w-w-want him to see the p-p-prize b-b-bullhead of the c-c-century."

Then I realized what had happened: my stammer had returned with a vengeance.

I stepped down to the slough edge to retrieve my catch. To my dismay every fish was gone. Each link which had once imprisoned a fish was empty. The stake which had anchored the stringer on the shore was now adorned with a beautiful grey and white feather tied in place with a bit of knotted reed.

I approached the feather. It certainly wasn't crow, hawk or gull, which were the kinds I occasionally picked up. I seemed to sense an energy flowing and singing inside me, just as I sometimes felt on Shaman's Point. I carefully removed it, and holding it gently by the shaft I carried the feather with me.

I passed through forest and field from Massacre Slough. I walked warily now that I knew the neighborhood was haunted by a fish thief.

As I approached the cabin, Tiny raced to greet me. Not far behind came my Hermit Uncle John. His face glowed in the setting sun. He looked like Moses after he'd received the Ten Commandments.

I started to spin out my terrible tale of the phantom fish stealer when, without a trace of stammer, he said, "Rog. I'm so glad you made it. I've been hopin' you'd come. Have I got a visitor for *you* to meet! He's a Sioux Indian shaman. That's a special holy man like those the Point was named for. I've mentioned him a time or two before. His name is Tony Great Turtle."

Before I could answer, he grabbed my hand and pulled me quickly toward the shack. We entered. Sitting in the main room in Uncle John's chair was the stranger from the slough shore. Pity Me lay on her back in his lap while he stroked her belly. He was still wearing his leather hat. There was one addition to its simplicity: a feather rose from its band which exactly matched the one whose shank I now clutched even more tightly in my right hand.

I stood stalk still in stark terror. Every tale of the warring Red Man I'd ever heard flashed across my mind-screen, especially the gory details invented by my family concerning my tomahawked great-granddaddy. All the terrible things I'd said about his people also scurried through my memory. Why had I foolishly shared another of my daddy's dark sides?

On the floor by the chair lay a beaded deerskin bag. Its motifs matched the arrowhead designs mounted around the walls. In the face of the unfamiliar and shattered by guilt over my terrible words, my imagination went rampant.

I thought I saw within the bag an outline of a sacrificial knife. Biblical images intermingled with memories of red fire. I had shuddered through Daily Vacation Bible School when, on the first day, we had been told the story of Abraham and

Isaac.

I knew what was going to happen to me. Through my shameful tale, I had revealed to the old man who I really was. I was the "no-good little bastard" impressed upon me by my daddy's whip and fist.

Under the cover of darkness the stranger, with assistance from the invisible but omnipresent "friends," would transport me to the tip of Shaman's Point and lay me on an ancient altar at the base of which the mysterious red fire flamed. Despite the tearful pleas of my Hermit Uncle John, the ritual blade would be raised. Unlike the Bible story there would be no substitutionary ram in the bushes.

The knife, reflecting the cold stars staring mercilessly down, would plunge into my tainted heart. The fire would instantaneously devour me. The west wind would blow my useless ashes away from the holy lake, depositing them at last on my father's fields.

Tony removed the feather from his hat and extended it toward me. I felt a strange tingling in my right hand. Perhaps it was simply from the tension of my nervous grip. I extended my feather and felt myself drawn slowly across the room.

The tips of our feathers touched. He whispered, "The sacred calls the sacred. It's good to be in touch."

I sank to the floor. It was as if every trace of fear and tension and pain I'd ever known flowed out of my body. He bent forward and gently removed the feather from my hand. For the first time a wry smile lighted his face.

He reached for the bag by his side. Pity Me slithered from his lap into mine. He placed one of the feathers inside and brought out, not a sacrificial knife, but an abalone shell which matched the one in my uncle's iris garden.

He said quietly, "All of us have darkness in us. We've got to be cleansed time and again."

At last I was on familiar ground. The sight of the abalone shell assured me. I would be taken outside. The old oak tub would be filled with sun-warmed water from the rain barrel.

I would lower myself into the water and Tony and Uncle John would each pour water over me with his abalone shell.

I was wrong. Tony Great Turtle began to chant a strange wordless rhythmic song not unlike those chanted by Gletha, the goatlady, in my woodland days in northern Minnesota. He withdrew from the bag two small deerskin pouches and some wooden matches. From one he sprinkled some dried leaves into the abalone shell. From the other he took a small twist of dried grass and dropped it into the shell. He replaced the pouches in the bag and returned it to the floor.

He struck a match on the rough underedge of the shell and touched it first to the leaves. They began to smolder. A rich, scented smoke arose. I recognized it at once. It smelled like the sage in my mother's Thanksgiving dressing. He lighted the twist of grass and intermingled it with the sage.

He quickly took the sacred feather and fanned the smudge until the smoke rose continuously in the darkening cabin. He held his hands within the smudging smoke. The chant changed. He directed the smoke to his head, his heart and then to his whole body.

My Hermit Uncle John stepped forward and received the smoking shell. He repeated the ceremony with such ease that I suspected he had done it many times before.

He then handed it to me. Tony's chant continued. Again my mind roamed. I had observed this once before. When a distant cousin had died, we went to her service in a Roman Catholic church. The robed priest had carried down the aisle a golden pot with smoke rising from it. He'd paused at the coffin and moved the smoking object over the deceased in a pattern similar to Tony's. Somehow, I felt reassured.

I received the feather and fanned the smudge into action. I passed the smoke across myself in the familiar pattern. I hoped my anger and fear would join the sacred cloud and disappear. The thought occurred to me that maybe I could borrow the necessary elements from Tony, and one day when my father was paralyzed by darkness I could smudge him and make him better.

I handed the warm abalone shell and the feather back to Tony. He held it for a long moment, breathing in the last vestiges of the rising smoke.

The sacred moment was broken by Pity Me who sneezed loudly and skittered from my lap and away from the final offending wisps rising from the cooling shell.

Tony broke off his chant with a chuckle. Uncle John lighted the bright-backed kerosene lamps. I became aware of other incense mingling with that from the abalone shell: frying chicken, fresh baked bread and the cinnamony perfume of apple pie.

Tony Great Turtle removed his hat. I noticed for the first time the neat braid of graying hair. We gathered at the laden table which had been set for three. Uncle John had obviously been assured that the sacred feather would draw me there. He said to me, "Why don't you say some words of blessing, Rog?"

We joined hands and I prayed the familiar, "Come, Lord Jesus; be our guest. And let this food to us be blessed. Amen." Again, I hadn't stammered, nor had my Uncle John.

Lifting his head, Tony said, "It's right that *all* holy ones be honored here."

I was ravenously hungry and thought we had sufficiently honored the holy ones, past and present. I reached for a crisp golden chicken leg, commenting as I did, "I'm sorry you had to chop the head off another rooster, Uncle John. I was going to bring you the biggest bullhead you ever saw in your whole life and five others almost as big but a fish thief...."

I stopped quickly, realizing that for the second time that day my tongue was racing ahead of my common sense.

Uncle John shook his head and responded, "I'm glad you didn't. You've been overloading me lately."

I glanced at Tony Great Turtle. He was staring at me intently. I could not break away from his eyes as he asked me, "Did you really *need* those fish?"

I whispered, "No."

He cut off my whisper with hard edged words, "That's why I released them. I watched you catch them. You never once gave thanks to the Great Spirit for those gifts from the water. You were doing it only for the joy of the kill.

"My people have starved because your people forgot that they are one with all people and killed our food only for the thrill of the hunt. A man received a name which became shameful to my people: Buffalo Bill."

I pricked up my ears. I'd paid a quarter for a heaping bushel basket full of books at a farm auction. Among the Horatio Alger's and Harold Bell Wright's were three falling-apart books by Ned Buntline all about Buffalo Bill. I'd never found anything shameful about him.

The old man continued, "When I was a little boy, William Cody shot 4,280 buffalo to feed the workers laying lines of railroad steel to tear our lands apart. They ate only the choice parts and left the rest to rot in the sun.

"Years later my father and I watched on a moonlit night as Cody won a bet. Someone called a Grand Duke had come from Europe and was riding the train across the plains. I later learned that they had been drinking together and Cody had bragged that he could kill one hundred buffalo with a hundred shots after nightfall. Feeling that it was a preposterous brag, the Grand Duke covered the bet of a thousand dollars.

"The train stopped in the midst of a herd of buffalo. We Indians had searched for food for days. These were the first of the great beasts we had seen. We were preparing to slip up to them and kill only what we could completely use. Men carrying lanterns rode their horses off the stock car at the end of the train and surrounded the herd. The lights reflected in the eyes of the buffalo.

"Cody fired into the left eye of a hundred startled buffalo. He never missed a shot. He and his men rode back onto the train. It disappeared into the darkness.

"My father wept. There was no way we could take care of so many fallen beasts. I think the Great Spirit wept as well."

My mind was working a mile a minute. I wanted to check out the truth of his story. I certainly did not want my hero's reputation darkened in any way. I had often dreamed of the handsome, bearded man pictured on Buntline's covers riding down our country road. He would sweep me into his saddle and carry me far beyond my mind sick daddy and milking cows and picking bugs off great fields of potato vines.

I asked, "But how did you learn about the bet?"

I glanced at my Hermit Uncle John. He was staring at me with his finger on his lips, signaling me to shush. It was too late.

The old man spoke in a voice edged with sadness. "Sometimes we do things we later regret. When I grew older, I wanted to escape from the reservation where we had been prisoners in our own land. William Cody needed Indians for his Wild West Show. The Bureau of Indian Affairs released a group of us. We traveled all over this country and Europe.

"Now I know that my people became looked upon by many as side show freaks rather than real people. The audiences in Madison Square Garden laughed and made gagging noises as we performed our 'dog eating' ceremony."

At the mention of such a ceremony I had a moment of anxiety for Tiny who was woofing quietly in her sleep as she curled on my feet.

He continued, "In England they cheered as Cody and his scouts littered the arena with 'dead' Indians and rescued 'captives' from 'savages' in the reenactment of the Battle of Summit Springs.

"When Buffalo Bill drank too much, he often bragged of killing the hundred buffalo and winning the bet."

Uncle John interrupted. "The food will be cold if we don't stop talking and start eating."

Tony Great Turtle wiped a tear from his cheek. A smile struggled to his face, and he took only what food he really needed from the various dishes.

At the end of the meal, the old man rose. I leaped to my

feet. I knew where we were going. We'd all go up to the tip of Shaman's Point. I could hardly wait to see what a real shaman might do.

Tony Great Turtle put on his hat and picked up his bag, saying, "I need to go to the great rock alone to be with myself and my people and the Great Spirit. I need to seek forgiveness in my own special ways."

He disappeared in the golden light of the sunset filtering through the branches of the black walnut tree.

"S-S-Someday he may even t-take us w-w-with him," my Uncle John said with longing in his voice.

I looked at the angle of the light, and the harsh reality of my situation overcame me: "I-I-I'm about an hour l-l-late t-to st-st-start the milking. My d-d-dad will skin m-m-me alive."

I dashed through the door and across the fields. I paused for a moment and looked back. In the gathering darkness red fire flared on Shaman's Point.

At that moment I realized a strange thing. When Tony Great Turtle left me and my Hermit Uncle John, our stammers returned.

Dear Gletha,

I met a most amazing man today—a Sioux Indian shaman called Tony Great Turtle. I wish the two of you could get together. With your powers from inside I bet you could rearrange the whole world and make it better.

He has a way of making a person look inside and see what's really there. That's kind of scary. I'm glad you had already started teaching me how.

Love,

Roger

Dear Rogee,

There's power for good and power for evil all around us. We both know that. I'm glad you've met somebody who seems to point you to deep journeying.

Your Uncle Dud says to me when I'm working on my herb salve, "Some days I think you're part Indian." That's one of the nicer things he says to me when he's awake enough to say anything at all.

The deep journey's got to go right with our stumbling along from place to place. Maybe we won't stumble quite so much.

I saw your cousin Stella today. You may find this hard to believe, but she's had a growth spurt and is just beautiful. I've about decided nothing is really ugly if you look at it hard enough—not even you, though you always thought yourself to be.

I've gone on too long. I've got to get this over to Jennie's.

Love,

Gletha

THE GRUBBER FISH

Lightning flared into the blasted oak, tearing away yet another limb. The dead giant stood proudly awaiting a second bolt, unwilling to succumb to the storm's fury. Perhaps I was not too late. If I stood beneath the tree, we could be destroyed together.

I huddled against the naked trunk. I felt a woodpecker's drumming inside the hollow core. Lightning ignited a straw stack in the next field. It smoldered in the torrential rain. I prayed to the God who haunted crosses, tombs and the granite tip of Shaman's Point that the next bolt would crumble the tree and me. My guilt, my shame, my worthlessness, my very memory would be erased.

I waited. The storm rumbled on as abruptly as it had arrived. A brilliant rainbow mocked me from the sky. The last thing I wanted was hope.

I turned bitterly away from the promised covenant in the heavens and slogged toward home through the deep muck of the freshly worked fields. At each step, my bare feet felt as if they were ooze-drawn toward the center of the earth. Perhaps if I stopped I would slowly sink into mud-smothered oblivion. Nobody would ever know what happened to me. At least I wouldn't have to be buried.

I waited. Great flocks of birds settled around me, capturing the angleworms driven to the surface by the downpour. The survivors could feast on me when they returned beneath the earth's surface.

I s-l-o-w-l-y sank in the rich loam—to a point midway between my ankles and my knees. I wiggled back and forth trying to resume my descent to the nether regions. It was to no avail. Wearily, I pulled out my right foot, set it before my left— and slogged on.

Struggling through the rain-washed world, I had plenty of time to consider the enormity of my recent action.

I had taken my Hermit Uncle John at his word. Whenever the violence of my father's mental illness erupted, or threatened to erupt, I would head for the sanctuary on the shore of Lake Sumach.

During my journey there I had to pass the Gundersons. This inevitably led to a painful interchange with George, Geoff and Giles, the Gunderson sons, aged nine, ten and eleven. Because of the common initial letter of their first names they called themselves the "G-Whizzes."

Their father, Glenn, was a huge, hearty, hard-drinking man. "A jack-of-all-trades and master of none," he was immensely proud of his boys.

Their mother, Willa, was a tiny, worn woman who repeatedly shared with anyone who would listen how bad each infant had torn her up as they clawed their way into the world. After the birth of Giles, she'd had "an operation." She just couldn't face the birth of another one.

Through the fluke of failed grades and being not quite a year apart in age, they ended up in the same school classroom. They terrorized recess activities. They cheated at games. They stole caps and choreographed elaborate patterns of "keep away."

The G-Whizzes were my personal nemeses. They led all the denizens of the playground in choric attacks of savage teasing. My terrible stammer was the center of their cruel attention. I was always chosen last for games. I had no close friends.

The boys would come at me and ask mockingly, "H-Hey, R-R-Roger, you w-w-wanna' p-p-play?"

There was nothing I wanted more in the whole world than to play. I'd smile as best I could and answer, "Y-Y-Yes. I'd l-l-like to p-p-play."

The children, led by the G-Whizzes, would turn away, their shrill laughter ringing in my ears. I would tuck my thumb into the bib pocket of my overalls and stroke my yellow teddy bear. The little creature who had lived there since the first Christmas after my adoption when I was four was always the still point of sanity in my turning world.

One day Giles discovered a tiny black kitten on the edge of the snowy playground. He put it in the huge pocket of his sheepskin coat. After recess, the coats were hung in a cloakroom like those adjacent to every classroom. The small room was used not only for garments and lunch buckets but also for the storage of supplies and as the locale for the eraser machine. Blackboard erasers were placed on its conveyer belt and magically pummeled free from chalk dust. It was also the place of discipline for students who transgressed the laws of the classroom. It became a second home for the G-Whizzes.

That afternoon, the three boys decided to transform the color of pink modeling clay by dumping the contents of an inkwell into the clay bucket. They were sent to the cloakroom.

Moments later the relative calm of the classroom was shattered by a feline shriek. Miss Lundeen, the teacher, was standing near the door. She flew into the cloakroom and grabbed for the small black kitten being held on the moving conveyor belt before the creature disappeared into the maw of the fateful machine.

The boys were again sent to Principal Jesse Moulter's office. Their father was again called. Arriving in his battered pickup truck, Glenn Gunderson lumbered into the school office. Principal Moulter was a tiny man whose chin scarcely cleared the high counter, giving him the appearance of a head knocked off in a *Punch and Judy* show battle.

Gunderson leaned intimidatingly above the principal. The G-Whizzes snickered on a bench behind him.

"Well, what have my boys thought up this time?"

Principal Moulter gave him a brief report. The father's responding roar of laughter could be heard all over the school. The boys' teachers, past, present and future, cringed.

Gunderson shouted, "Well, Jesse, boys will be boys. When you gonna' git yerself some teachers which kin hold my kids' attention?"

Turning to his admiring sons, he said, "C'mon, guys. We'll stop for the usual and then head out on old Lake Sumach. I hear tell the ice's thick enough to do a little fishing."

As they turned to leave, Geoff thumbed his nose at the frightened face floating above the counter edge.

Myrtle Weedon, who worked the soda fountain in Pruden's Drugstore, later reported that they'd paused and had triple dip black walnut ice cream cones all around. Whenever the boys were sent home from school, they were treated to triple dip black walnut ice cream cones—whatever the weather. The Gundersons were among her most frequent customers.

On a hot day just after school let out for the summer, I was lazily pulling pigweeds out of the pea patch. I was watching the clouds draw pictures in the sky more intently than I was watching what I was doing.

His voice cut through my reverie: "What the hell do you think you're doing, kid?"

My father loomed over me as I knelt on the sun-baked earth. From his hand dangled two pea vines which I had accidentally pulled along with the encroaching weeds.

I had no time to duck. His open hand slammed into the side of my head. I toppled from my kneeling position face forward across the row, flattening more vines than he held in his hand. My face ground into the manure we'd spread as fertilizer.

As he turned to leave, he barked, "Maybe you'll remember next time to pay attention to what you're doing."

As he walked down the row, I noticed the increasing stoop

in his shoulders. That was a sure sign that he was slipping into a darkness. It looked like it was time for another visit to my Hermit Uncle John's.

I tried to move quickly past the Gundersons', hoping to go unnoticed. George, Geoff and Giles came racing down upon me.

They shouted together, "Hey, R-R-Roger, you wanna' play?"

I was lonely. I thought maybe without the audience of our classmates they might have decided to be decent and include me.

I replied as best I could, "Y-Y-Yeah, I'd l-l-like to p-p-play."

Geoff responded, "We was playing on the front porch, and we saw Mrs. Williams across the road set out three apple pies to cool on her porch railing. We'd really like one of those pies. Go steal us one. Then you can play with us."

I wanted to play in the worst way. I didn't want to do it that way. I responded, "N-N-No, I've b-b-been t-t-taught not t-to st-st-steal."

Geoff responded derisively, "What's the matter, boy? Ain't you got no balls?"

George continued the sequence, "Of course he ain't got no balls. He ain't got nothin' between his legs."

Giles finished off with, "I'll bet he's just a dumb girl. Let's take his pants down and find out."

I fled. Only their demonic laughter pursued me.

I was glad when Shaman's Point rose up above the countryside. It heralded closeness, caring and deep-running mystery.

As I walked through the woods to the shack, I smelled the aroma of fresh baked bread. Something leaped into the path directly in front of me. I started like a frightened pheasant. It was Tiny. I squatted down and the little fox terrier leaped into my arms, quivering with the sheer joy of my arrival. Then, springing to the ground, she dashed around in small circles as she led me up the path toward the shack. As we drew nearer, I called out my uncle's name. He stepped outside and welcomed me with a hug.

He held me at arm's length. "You should have washed your f-f-face before you came."

"I was doing a l-l-little rooting in the manure of the pea patch. I left k-k-kind of quick."

He didn't respond. He simply led me into the house. He filled the washbasin on the kitchen shelf with warm water from the stove's reservoir. He gently washed my face—then sat me down and served me warm bread and milk. Tiny didn't even bother going to her box in the corner. She curled up on my bare feet.

As I finished my repast, Uncle John said with exaggerated casualness, "I was hoping you'd c-c-come by one of these days soon. I've been wanting to introduce you to my n-n-new friend."

My Uncle John had a friend? I thought I was the only person in the whole world he spent any real time with.

"Where does your new f-f-friend live?" I asked.

"Down b-b-by the lake."

"But there ain't no other houses anywhere n-n-near here, and I know you don't usually w-w-wander around very far when you don't have to."

"J-J-Just you wait and see. My new friend doesn't need a house," he added mysteriously.

I gulped down my last bit of bread and milk. Uncle John had gone to the bread drawer, removed a loaf and tucked it into the huge pocket of his worn jacket.

"Are we going to have l-l-lunch with your friend?" I queried.

"Don't ask so m-m-many questions. Just wait and see."

As we stepped outside, Uncle John said, "We may as well take our cane p-p-poles and worm can. I'm about out of bullheads. We can fish after you m-m-meet my friend."

"Does your f-f-friend have his own pole, or should we take

one for him?"

Uncle John grinned broadly. "He doesn't n-n-need a pole."

Under the excited leadership of Tiny we arrived at the lakeshore. The granite tip of Shaman's Point loomed above us. Having made Tiny sit well back from the lake, we walked out onto a large rock which, at water's edge, sloped gently down into the lake. Uncle John had told me that the Indians once launched their canoes from here. It was an ideal place for us to fish for fat bullheads, sunfish and crappies.

I placed my feet carefully to avoid the knife-like ridges which ribbed the surface of the launching site.

At one side of the rock a crystal clear spring bubbled up into a pool which was joined to the lake through a narrow neck of water. Uncle John knelt down by the spring fed pool, took the bread out of his pocket and laid it on the rock beside him.

"Hey!" I exclaimed, "N-N-Nobody's going to want to eat that beautiful bread after it's l-l-laid there on the rock where we've cleaned fish and stuff."

"You'll b-b-be surprised," he said, grinning up at me.

He was staring into the depths of the pond. He slapped its surface slowly three times with the palm of his hand. Then he lowered his hand gently into the water.

I stepped to his side just in time to see a big, fat mossy-backed carp swim up to his hand. He seemed to be stroking the great, ugly fish down its finny spine. The fish was twisting in the water like a pussycat.

Then my Uncle John began breaking off large pieces of the bread and dropping them on the surface of the water. The fish stuck out its snout and scarfed down the bread. Sometimes Uncle John would submerge the bread. The fish would take it from his fingers.

I was dumbfounded!

"Uncle John, l-l-let me feed some bread to the fish."

"Oh, no! This old grubber f-f-fish spooks easy. You've got to let him get used to you. Just kneel d-d-down here by me and put your hand gently in the water."

At the entry of my hand, the fish swam quickly away through the neck of water and out into the lake.

Awestruck that Uncle John had tamed a wild thing, I asked, "How did you meet up with your n-n-new friend, the grubber fish, Uncle John?"

"I had my line out one d-d-day at high noon. There was a ray of sunlight dancing on the spring pond. I saw something moving l-l-lazily in the w-w-water. I thought at first it was a m-m-muskrat. Then I saw it was an enormous old carp. I'd brought a c-couple of sandwiches with me. I moved slowly and placed a bit of bread on the s-s-surface of the water. The old gr-gr-grubber fish made a gr-gr-grab for it, then swished away to the other side of the little pond. I put another b-b-bit of bread in the water. He swam back close to the surface. His backfin c-c-cut the water like a shark's. It was then that I saw how big he was. He l-l-looked as old as the lake itself.

"He didn't grab as fast for the b-b-bread this time. He hung around my side of the pond. I gave him the rest of my sandwich. I held the final bit in my thumb and f-f-finger and lowered my hand s-l-o-w-l-y into the water. The old fish sort of nuzzled the bread out of my gr-gr-grip.

"In the p-p-process I think he brushed across my th-th-thumbnail. He seemed to like the feeling and swam back and forth a c-c-couple of times. Maybe I was dislodging some tiny parasites from his scales.

"I started coming d-d-down every day at the same time. Sometimes he wasn't there. I tried p-p-putting bread in the water to draw him—but the minnows and the little sunfish always t-t-took it first. It was then that I started to g-g-gently slap the water. At first he didn't seem to c-c-catch on. B-B-But I don't have a lot to do, so I just kept at it.

"All of a sudden he s-s-seemed to understand. Now he comes almost every time I call him any time of the d-d-day or night. Oh, once in a while he's gone for a day or two. I think he m-m-must go on some sort of p-p-pilgrimage to the other end of the lake. He's become real good c-c-company. We sort of understand one another.

"The other n-n-night when the m-m-moon was full I came down, c-c-called him and p-put bread in the water. He came qu-qu-quickly and scarfed it down. I tickled him along his finny spine.

"Then, all of a sudden, I saw a l-l-light glowing on the tip of the great rock. The grubber fish turned. I swear he c-c-could s-s-see it too. He became absolutely motionless. Then he started t-t-to swim in a graceful circle around the edge of the p-pool. It was as if he was doing some k-kind of dance. He swam past me seven times. Then he d-d-disappeared. I decided right then that he had to be some k-k-kind of King of this Holy Lake.

"I've really grown to l-l-love that old fish. It feels good to have four friends now: Tiny, Pity Me, the gr-gr-grubber fish and you. Some days I do think the grubber fish is the b-b-best friend I've ever had."

His eyes twinkled as he spoke.

Tiny had pricked up her ears when her name was mentioned. The small, folded-in man—still shadowed by his great height, if you looked close—whistled for the dog. She came bounding across the rock, her toenails making a scraping rhythm as she ran. He surrounded her with his arms.

"D-D-Don't worry, Tiny. A person can really l-l-love more than one living thing at a time."

Weeks passed. Each time I fled from my father's anger to the symboled grotto on the lakeshore, we visited the King of the Holy Lake. I was eager to call, feed and stroke the fish. Uncle John refused. The carp was a sacred part of the lake. Though we offered him bread, his coming to us was a gift. Sometimes as I stood by, watching Uncle John caress the fish, I thought I saw it eying me appraisingly.

One day after a minor whipping I headed for the shack on the lake. The words that my daddy used had hurt worse than the green willow branch. He was probably right. I really was "no damn good." Not even the bear in my bib could make it any better.

The Gunderson boys descended like biblical locusts. I was feeling bad enough about myself. I didn't want to deal with them.

George shouted, "Hey, Roger! Wait a minute. We *really* want you to play with us. We need a fourth person to even teams so we can play Auntie-I-Over at the garage."

He sounded friendly. Maybe they had grown up over the summer. I was beginning to feel better already. Maybe I wouldn't need to go to Uncle John's after all.

They clustered around me, awaiting my answer.

After a moment's hesitation I responded, "Yeah, th-th-thanks. I'll b-be g-g-glad to even t-t-teams."

Geoff cut in, "While we find the ball and get some stuff picked up so we can run better, we got a little job for you. Last night the wind carried the sweetest smell on this whole earth into our bedroom window. And we knew right off that Hattie Holly's muskmelons were ripe. You sneak over and get us a couple. We'll bury them in the icehouse. After we've played for a while, we'll have ourselves some nice, cool muskmelon."

Hattie Holly's garden was legendary. She always got county fair blue ribbons for her produce. She lived alone. She had a gold star in her window for her son killed in France. Then her husband had died when a storm overturned his boat on Lake Sumach. He couldn't swim. She'd had enough things happen. I was not about to steal from her. I turned and walked quickly toward my Uncle John's.

Thinking they were well on their way toward their garage, I didn't hear them sneak up behind me. Giles and Geoff each grabbed an arm. George grabbed my feet. They swung me in the air face down.

George jeered: "Hey, R-R-Roger. Th-Th-That wasn't the w-w-way to Mrs. Holly's m-m-m-melon patch."

His brothers roared at his imitation.

I cried out, "I-I-I t-told you b-b-before, I-I-I d-don't steal st-st-st-stuff."

Giles said, "We let you get away before. But we've got you this time. Hey, guys, should we take the pants off of old lady, scairdy-cat Rog?"

"Naw," sneered George, "he ain't got nothin' hangin' worth seein'. Let's not waste our time. Let's just drop him in a fresh cow pie."

The Gunderson's cattle grazed quietly around us. My tormentors wouldn't have to look far. I quickly found myself suspended over a pile of still-steaming, soft manure. They held me close enough to the ground so that when they dropped me I could not catch myself with my hands and avoid the catastrophe.

They let go. My face plunged into the fetid mound. They ran, screaming with laughter, into their overgrown orchard.

I pulled some tall grass and wiped as much as I could from my face and out of my hair. Then I ran through the woods to the rock-sheltered shack.

I burst through the front door. My Uncle John was curled up in his big chair reading *The Decline and Fall of the Roman Empire*. Tiny was asleep in her box.

Without a word he took me to the kitchen. He set the washpan on the floor. I stripped my overalls down to my waist. I knelt by the pan. Once again he washed my hair and face with his homemade soap. The aroma of wintergreen quickly overcame the pungent smell of cow dung.

When my ablutions were complete, I told him what had happened.

His only comment was, "B-B-Barbarian attacks are not limited to Rome."

Then he continued: "I have a feeling that this is probably the d-d-day. Having gone through that special initiation r-r-rite in the cow p-p-pasture, I think you can properly become a courtier to the King of the Lake."

We both laughed. My heart soared. Uncle John was finally trusting me to feed his best friend in the whole world.

I marched to the bread drawer in the kitchen cabinet and removed an extra large piece of the high-risen delicacy. As I stepped back into the living room, I noticed that a new panel had been added to the wall covering. Resplendent against the intricately woven dried reeds was the outline of a great fish traced in arrowheads.

We picked up our cane poles. A fearful thought occurred to me: "Uncle John, we shouldn't really f-f-fish right after we've fed your friend. What if, as he swims away, he grabs one of the worms we've strung on the hooks. We c-c-could hurt him something terrible."

"Don't worry," he responded. "C-C-Carp seldom pay any attention to worms. When they start to run in the springtime, I always spear a f-f-few to hang in the smokehouse. However, I doubt the royal grubber fish would ever eat a lowly worm."

"What do you think he eats, Uncle John?"

"Why, deep purple water lily p-p-petals in summer and pure, white papyrus roots in winter."

I looked at him in sheer wonderment at the breadth of his knowledge. There was a quizzical look in his eye. He might have been teasing me—but with all those books on the shelf I was certain he knew just about everything there was to know in the whole world.

Tiny led us to the great flat rock. I stepped out onto it gingerly in order to protect my feet. We laid down our poles. Tiny sat obediently by them.

I quickly moved to the side of the clear, spring fed little pond. I knelt. My heart was pounding in anticipation.

I held up the bread in my left hand. No priest ever elevated the host with more majesty. I slapped the water three times with my right hand. After a moment the great fish swam into the middle of the pond. He paused there for a moment, sensing a difference in procedure. Then he swam slowly toward me.

I floated a piece of the bread on the water. The grubber fish nosed it for a moment, then ate it with his usual voraciousness. I held the second piece under the water. He ate it from my hand.

I held my fingers under the water. The old fish swam up to them. I stroked along his backfin. I put both hands in the water. He rubbed against them, moving like a pussycat. He seemed to particularly like my hands underneath him, stroking the smoother skin.

I looked up at my Uncle John. He was smiling. There were ghosts of tears in his eyes. I could tell he was proud of me.

Having fed and stroked the grubber fish, we stepped to the other side of the rock, baited our hooks and threw them out. They scarcely hit the water before the bobbers on the ends of our lines ducked beneath the surface.

They didn't stop. We caught more fish in a shorter period of time than ever before. It was as if the King of the Deep had brought members of his court to be sacrificed for his benefit so that he might continue to be gifted with bread and touch.

As the days passed, I would visit Uncle John not only because of pain at home but so that I too could call forth the mysterious carp. The G-Whizzes were always present. Having performed what for them was the ultimate humiliation, their torment now was nonphysical. They echoed my father's themes concerning my general worthlessness. I wished they would remain silent and strike me. It might have been easier.

I quickly learned what the grubber fish liked most—beyond my Uncle John's magnificent bread. I'd put my hands underneath him and rock him up and down in the water like a carousel pony. I'd do it a few times and then remove my hands. He would float in the water as if he were in a trance. After a few moments he would slowly swim away, scarcely moving a fin.

On a Saturday morning in early fall, my father came to the breakfast table, his shoulders hunched, his face set. It was obvious that he was heading into one of his darknesses. It was evident as well that he knew what was ahead. He needed to finish certain tasks before the depression imprisoned him in his creaky living room rocking chair.

I hunkered down over my pancakes and eggs, hoping he

wouldn't notice me. He looked at me and announced, "I need some work out of you today, kid. I don't want you kitin' off, spending the day at the lake with that crazy brother of mine. I want to finish the southeast field. I plowed about half of it yesterday afternoon. I'll take the tractor and finish the plowing.

"Before I go, I'll hitch Buster and Judy to the drag. You can smooth it all out after me. The soil is nice and soft this fall. I'm not going to have to break up the clods with the disk first. That sure saves us some work."

I cringed. I was afraid of the huge plowhorses. Buster delighted in sneaking up behind me in the pasture and nipping my neck. He was a terribly nervous animal. He shied at the slightest movement. I was skinny and weak. I knew I was never in control.

The great matched team of Belgian workhorses was the source of my father's deepest pride. He spent hours currycombing their sleek, brown sides. Sometimes during harvest he'd drive them into the elevator with a wagonload of grain just to get the admiring comments of the gathered farmers, most of whom used tractors and trucks to do their hauling. He was careful to pad their harnesses so that there would be no worn places in their glistening coats.

He shared the story over and over again with anyone who would listen of how he'd driven the team to town while a circus was playing. The foreman in charge of the menagerie had stopped him and offered him an incredible amount of money for his matched pair. He wanted them to pull the gold-appointed lion wagon in parades. However, Dad told the man he wouldn't take a million dollars for this team.

I heard him comment once to the admiring circle of listeners, "Any man who ever does anything to scar one of my horses is as good as dead."

Having finished our breakfast, we headed for the barn-yard. I helped harness the beasts as best I could. Dad's nerves were getting tighter and tighter as he readjusted everything I did.

We walked the horses through tall alfalfa to the south field on the edge of which lurked the great drag: two huge iron squares with evenly spaced teeth which tore up the sod turned over by the plow. Dad hitched the horses to the ungainly piece of equipment. He drove the horses and their burden to a starting position on the freshly plowed field.

He handed me the long reins which, of necessity, extended behind the sprawling drag. He gave me a final instruction: "Make sure you overlap your strips. Any outsize clods will throw the corn planter off when I seed in the spring."

Without another word he returned to start the tractor in the barnyard.

I shouted, "Giddap" to the horses. They stood there a moment without moving. They let me know exactly who was in charge. Then they lumbered off down the field at their own pace. I decided to experiment halfway down the field. I shouted, "Whoa!" With great disdain Judy looked over her shoulder at me. In common conspiracy, the two horses kept moving.

As we came back down the field, I carefully overlapped the strips. We were facing the barnyard. I could hear Dad swearing at the old Fordson tractor, an ever reluctant morning starter. There were dissonant clangs as, in his exasperation, he slammed whatever tool he had at hand into the heavy fenders of the machine.

I started to laugh as I remembered the morning when Mom and I were picking cucumbers in the garden. Dad was trying to start the tractor. He had a monkey wrench in his hand. In the depths of his anger he slammed the wrench into the Fordson's fender. It broke in two. He stared in bewilderment at the handle still clutched in his fist. The blackly comic enormity of the situation overcame my mother. She burst into laughter. A shamefaced grin broke over Dad's face. He came toward her. He let go an immense bellylaugh and took her in his arms. Such a display of happy affection between them was rare.

He was not laughing this morning. From a distance I could hear indistinguishable shouts. I had been close often enough to know that endless combinations of profanity were filling the air. Sometimes when I was near him I'd swear, using some of his richer combinations. If he was not in a darkness, he'd smile and say, "Maybe you'll grow up to be a man yet."

I was relieved when the engine started and the old machine coughed its way toward the field.

Though I was not looking forward to a day of monotony behind the plodding steeds, I was proud of how straight was my strip of smooth soil—how well overlapped.

I was about to wave to him as he drove past me twenty yards away. At that moment a pheasant which had been crouching in a furrow exploded into the air practically under Buster's chin. He reared and leaped to the left. The right hand section of the drag flipped up. In the confusion Judy backed slightly. As the drag crashed back to the earth, a steel tooth scraped a short, shallow gash down her flank.

I stood absolutely petrified, the reins slack in my hands, letting the horses do whatever they would to right themselves.

My father stopped the tractor, leaped off and came running across the field. He grabbed the slack reins from my hands. With incredible strength and sheer willpower he jerked the horses into submission. He headed them in the proper direction.

He turned on me. The expected slap 'side the head came with more force than usual. The air was filled with profanity, surpassing his usual responses to a reluctant tractor. Woven into the swearing were slashes of his verbal stiletto which shredded any sense of self-worth. My thumb strayed to the bib pocket of my overalls. It stroked the soft, accepting surface of the resident bear.

Dad rehearsed how many times he had told me *never* to allow a loose rein with Buster and how the whole accident was really my fault—not the horse's or the pheasant's.

He grabbed the front of my overalls to pull me closer to him. The bib snap gave way. The occupant was revealed. The stream of abuse cut off midword. He grabbed the small, worn bear, stared at it in disbelief and threw it as hard as he could toward the unplowed field. My heart followed the bear's slow arc, then plunged with it to the earth. A deep hatred for the raging man flowed into the emptiness inside left by my absent talisman.

He turned to me and said somewhat wistfully, "How did that orphanage ever manage to give me such a spineless sissy for a son?"

It was then that he noticed the gash on Judy's flank. I thought I had, over the years, experienced the heights and depths of my father's anger. But I knew the explosion that was about to come would be unique. Someone had scarred his perfect horse.

It was the shallowest of wounds. It was black with flies. He walked over to the tractor, opened a greasecock, took out a fingerful of the dark brown lubricant and gently rubbed it on Judy's flank to discourage the marauding insects.

The silence was deafening. If he'd just scream or swear or slap me. I knew what he'd do when he finished ministering to his horse. He would "help me remember what to do next time." This always involved a systematic beating. I thought I may as well get ready for it.

I slipped off my overalls, being careful to keep one hand over my privates in case he looked around. I huddled down in a deep furrow as the pheasant had done. I wished I could fly away—forever.

I became strangely analytical. What instrument would he use to underscore my memory? Perhaps he'd pull a dead branch from the lightning-blasted oak in the center of the field. Would he be content to use his bare hand, the callous-hardened palm slamming again and again into the soft flesh of my bare buttocks? Or would he use the end of the leather reins to raise long, red welts on my exposed flesh? I carefully covered my head with my arms.

I waited for an interminable time. There was no sound except for the clink of the harnesses as the horses tried to keep away the determined flies.

I felt some drops of water fall on me. Had it begun to sprinkle? I spread my fingers and looked up. My father was standing above me, tears cascading down his cheeks and onto my womb-positioned body in the furrow.

Wordlessly, he turned away, unhitched the horses and drove them back to the barn. I lay there for a long time, waiting for this fresh revelation to sink in: I was too worthless to be taught anything. I was beyond beating. There was simply no self left.

I heard a soft, thumping sound. I looked up to see a great jack rabbit leap over the furrow in which I lay. Not even the animals of the fields took any notice of me.

I slowly uncurled myself from the black earth. I slipped on my overalls, snapped the bib pocket shut and started off toward Lake Sumach. Perhaps Uncle John and the sacred fish could help me find me again. I looked over my shoulder at my father. He was watching me closely. In case I ever wanted to come home, I'd better make no effort to find the bear.

I stumbled across the rough plowed field, feeling terrible about myself—which is the worst thing you can ever feel terrible about. I passed the Gundersons. The G-Whizzes were nowhere to be seen. Strangely enough, I was sorry. I was filled with an absolutely overwhelming desire to play with somebody. I was feeling so bad that I would give anything to play with another living being who might make me feel like somebody.

I walked up the path toward the shack, keeping a wary eye out for Tiny whose silent jumping out at me had become her favorite game. She was nowhere in sight.

I called for my Hermit Uncle John. He didn't answer. I walked into the cabin. It was empty.

I really needed somebody. I knew he wouldn't mind if I

visited the grubber fish. I went to the kitchen bread drawer. I took out a good sized piece of bread and headed for the lakeshore.

I stepped out on the big, sloping rock, being careful to place my feet between the sharp ridges. Moving to the edge of the spring pool, I knelt down and slapped the water three times. In a moment the grubber fish swam majestically through the opening from Lake Sumach. At least the King of the Sacred Lake still considered me worthy of kneeling at his table. Or did he see me only as source of a delicacy?

I held some bread under water. The great fish nibbled it daintily. I floated a larger piece on the surface. The carp gulped it while passing casually. I held a final piece under water. He finished it off.

I kept my hand under the water. He swam languidly back and forth, rubbing himself against it. I scratched my thumbnail along his backfin. He wiggled like a pussycat.

I put my other hand in the water and stroked his rough-scaled stomach. I began to move him gently up and down in the water like a figure on a carousel. He was perfectly mesmerized, immobile.

I began to think, "He's nothing but an old fish—the only thing a no-good boy's got to play with."

At that moment I felt something watching me. Was it something real—or just some of Uncle John's good friends from Shaman's Point. I turned my head slowly. There stood George and Geoff and Giles eying me in silent awe. George laid down the heavy stick he was carrying. They squatted on either side of me as I continued to cradle the great fish.

Giles said softly, "Wow! We've been watching your dumb, old uncle with that dumb, old fish, but we didn't know you could touch him too. What are you—magic or something?"

Geoff smiled at me, put a surprisingly gentle hand on my shoulder and asked, "Hey, Rog: would you like to come and play with us?"

His brothers nodded their assent to his request.

I couldn't believe it. He had asked me without mocking me. They were admiring something I was doing. It was exactly the invitation I needed to make me feel like somebody again.

"S-S-Sure. I'd l-l-like to p-play with y-y-you."

They smiled as though pleased at the mere thought that I was going to play with them.

George continued softly, "We'd really like to have *you* play with *us*, Rog. Just give us that dumb, old carp, and you can play with us."

Not a thought crossed my mind. I was overcome by the possibility that I might be real again. I'd feel good about me if I could just play with somebody.

With one mighty heave I flipped the majestic old fish out of the crystal water and onto the harsh surface of the launching rock.

The boys leaped to their feet with a shrill, choric yell: "Whoope-e-e-e! We've got the dumb, old fish!"

They began dancing around the grubber fish. He was flopping with all his might, instinctively straining to get back into the water. Each time he hit the rock, one of the sharp ridges would cut into his flesh. The boys kept kicking him toward the center of the rock.

On one kick George cut the soft flesh on the top of his foot with one of the bony fins. He cried out in pain, "That damned old fish just cut me. I'll fix him."

I crouched in frozen terror as he picked up the heavy stick he'd been carrying and lifted it high in the air. He brought it down on the head of the old grubber fish. The King of the Holy Lake lay there, motionless.

The boys looked down at the limp body of the carp. Geoff commented, "Ugh—what good is a dead, old, ugly fish to anybody?"

George dropped his stick. The G-Whizzes disappeared into the underbrush, giggling hysterically.

I unfolded slowly. I crawled across the rock. The knife-like ridges slashed at my hands and knees. I collapsed by the lifeless, lacerated body of my Uncle John's best friend in the whole world, the King of the Holy Lake.

I had come to the lakeside to try and discover something alive, something worthwhile in me. I thought I was absolutely dead inside. I was wrong. I discovered a deeper sense of meaninglessness with the death of the grubber fish.

I had to get away. I couldn't face my Uncle John. The emptiness inside was quickly filling with guilt and self-loathing.

I had to deal with the body of my friend who had trusted me absolutely. I picked him up. A horsefly landed on one of his great eyes over which the film of death was forming. I walked across the rock and up the path through the underbrush.

I was drawn upward toward Shaman's Point. I climbed the great outcropping and laid the stiffening body on the very edge of the sheer cliff. I wanted to throw myself down to the rocks on the lakeshore below. I didn't have the courage.

I hoped somebody or something would tell me what to do next. The sky was clouding in the distance. Faraway lightning tore the heavens. I looked from the rock and saw the great oak under which Uncle John buried the human bones he found in his garden. I knew what I had to do.

I carried the fish down the narrow path, scrambled across the clearing and laid the carp's body under the tree. I went back to the shack and picked up a long-nosed shovel from the adjoining toolshed.

Returning to the tree, I dug a grave for the great fish. With my last shovelful of dirt I unearthed a tiny skull. It must have belonged to a child. I laid my friend in the black earth and nestled the skull against the fish's head. I didn't want him to be lonely. Maybe the spirit of that child would treat him better than I had. I gently covered them both with soft earth, moistened by my tears.

The thunder, lightning and rain hit with a ferocity unusual even for that storm-haunted country. As the sheets of flame danced over Lake Sumach, I began running through the torrents toward the dead tree in the middle of our freshly cultivated field. It always drew fire from heaven. If I was incinerated, maybe my spirit could join the grubber fish and I could make amends. Perhaps I might play with the Indian child forever.

The rainbow came too early. I was damned to wander alive and lost.

I could see our house in the distance. Dad had finished the work in the field before the rains hit. I knew he would be slumped in his chair in a deep depression. I would be left with all the milking and hog feeding. Maybe Mom would have at least gathered the eggs and fed the chickens.

I wanted to talk to somebody. I wanted to unload the guilt over what I had done. Ahead of me a flash of yellow marred the expanse of tilled black earth. I slogged toward it. It was an arm of my old yellow bear. I dug the earth from around him, not wanting to pull lest he'd been torn by the plow or the drag. He was intact.

I knelt in the mud, cradled this muddy toy friend in my arms and wept. I shared the entire story with the bear. Not even the sheen of mud could eliminate the glow of understanding in his remaining eye. I continued my journey toward the tiny, paint-peeling house. The bear was again snapped safely in his pocket nest.

My mother was nowhere to be seen. The only sound was the rhythmic creak of my father's chair as he rocked out the pattern of his depression.

I stepped outside and dipped a pail of water from the rain barrel. I plunged my stained bear in it again and again. He quickly returned to his usual yellow-grey state. I took a clothespin and hung him by his ear on the drying line. The late afternoon sun was beating down with a particular intensity now that the rain had subsided.

I finished my round of chores. I heard the screen door slam and knew that my mother had returned. The air was torn with the shriek of a young rooster captured by a wire hook on a long stick. This was followed by the dull thud of an ax on the chopping block and the smell of feathers dipped in boiling water to loosen them for plucking. I knew we would have fried chicken for supper. I also knew why. When my father was happy and Mom fried chicken, he always commented that the smell would bring anybody back from the dead. That's where he was now.

I brought in the milk, left it for Mom to run through the separator with her steady, practiced hand and washed up. I moved through the routine automatically, unthinking. All I sensed was a hole torn in the center of my soul by my evil deed of that afternoon.

I washed up and came to the table. My father sat in his usual place, staring into space. Mom set down the platter of golden chicken, placing a thigh and a breast on his plate along with a baked potato and fresh garden peas. She cut up his food as if he were a child. She placed a spoon in his hand. He ate slowly.

I nibbled around the edges of my supper, eating just enough so that my mother would ask no questions. We didn't talk. We were each walled into our particular world of grief.

Catching my mother's eye, I excused myself from the table with a look and stepped outside. A sliver of a moon and a million stars rose over the eastern edge of the trees as the western sky darkened. I rescued my still-damp bear from the clothesline and stepped into my room.

I stripped. In the darkness I picked up my copy of *Twenty Thousand Leagues Under the Sea* hidden behind the door. I wanted to read by flashlight under the covers: an act absolutely forbidden by my father. Since I had already committed the ultimate sin in the death of the grubber fish, I laid the book aside. I couldn't bear any additional guilt. I lighted my little kerosene lamp. I looked into the cracked mirror. Everything about me seemed shriveled. Had my father been present, I would not have needed to hide my privates. Gripping my damp bear, I scurried under the covers of my bed without bothering with the worn pajamas. I flopped on my stomach and buried my head in my pillow.

All night I wove in and out of the same dream. I was standing naked up to my neck in the crystal spring pool by the launching rock. My arms were bound to my sides by long strands of waterweed. The grubber fish swam slowly, endlessly around me. I could see his lacerated sides. His eyes never left mine.

Above me loomed Shaman's Point. A small Sioux boy stared down at me from the great rock. I became dizzy and nauseated. I cried out to the ancient fish to stop. He kept swimming. I didn't want to soil the surrounding pool with my vomit. I kept fighting it down. Dozens of small fish nibbled gently at my fingertips, the ends of my toes, my nipples and the bare head of my penis. Every muscle in my body grew taut with the touch of pleasure and the fear of pain.

I awakened. I felt totally debilitated. The sheet between my legs was soaked by the wet dream's ejaculate. The rest of the bed was dampened with perspiration. The nausea could no longer be contained. I stumbled out the back door beneath the cold stars. My body was torn by terrible retching. The grey geese, awakened by my activity, crowded around to cannibalize the bits of undigested fried chicken.

I returned to my bed, determined to remain awake for the rest of the night. I could not endure further contact with the images. In spite of myself, I fell into sleep. The pattern repeated itself again. Finally, my gut convulsing with dry heaves, I stood naked under the staring eye of Venus, the morning star. The eastern sky was touched by the first rays of light. I could not vomit out my guilt.

I reentered my room, pulled on a clean pair of overalls, carefully snapped my damp bear into the bib pocket and stumbled weakly toward the barn to do the morning chores.

I moved through the day in a daze. I took a small can of kerosene and flipped potato bugs into it from the vines near the garden. Maybe if I killed enough destructive living things, I could somehow propitiate for having caused the death of the encrusted ugly fish who somehow in my mind was Love alive.

It didn't work. I knew there was only one course open to me. I had to return to my Hermit Uncle John's—not because of a beating from my father but because of continual self-laceration which I had no power to stop.

I had read somewhere that totally evil beings cast no shadow. In the intense heat of the September sun, I looked behind me. I was casting no shadow. I took no notice of the fact that the sun was directly overhead. I knew I had to do something or I might cause an even more disastrous event to occur—if such a thing were possible.

As I came near the Gunderson's, I saw George and Geoff and Giles playing catch in their front yard. There was no way I could deal with them on any level. So intent were they on their game they didn't spot me. I dove into the nearest ditch. I avoided rolling all the way to the bottom where water stood from yesterday's downpour. A stand of cattails grew there from the frequent moisture.

I lay motionless. I noticed the ridged eyes of a giant bullfrog rise slowly out of the water and rotate in his constant vigil for food. A few inches away a garter snake gleamed in the filtered sunlight. A huge grasshopper alighted on a leaf between the waiting animals, touches of turquoise and red on wing and torso brought alive in the light. Simultaneously, two long, sticky tongues shot out toward the insect as it rocketed upward to continue its journey. It was not given even a moment to celebrate its deliverance before disappearing into the beak of a swooping redwinged blackbird. The bird arced gracefully to a nearby willow and warbled a song of thanksgiving. I only wished that a giant bird would sweep down and carry me off into some kind of oblivion, free from my terrible interior pain.

I heard a high-pitched cry of fear. I peered through the grass toward the Gunderson's front yard. The boys were not playing with a ball. They were tossing, albeit gently, their six-week-old collie puppy from one to the other. The little beast was howling piteously, paralyzed with fright.

Hearing the sound, Willa Gunderson swept out of the house, caught the puppy in mid-air and cradled it in her arms. It burrowed under the bib of her apron.

Her only action toward the boys was to point to the house and utter three brief, crystal clear commands: "Giles: churn. Geoff: dishes. George: wood."

Their complaints rang out in the order of the commands: "Aw, Ma: we weren't hurtin' the pup." "Yeah, Ma: he really likes our attention." "Geez, Ma: we were only funnin'."

Willa remained silent but continued to snuggle the puppy safely—and to point. The boys moped their way into the house. Soon the sound of the slow chop of George's axe, of Geoff attacking the dishes with such angry force that their survival was in question and the reluctant grind of Giles's churn assured me that I could drag my scared, scarred self out of the ditch toward an unknown resolution of events at my Hermit Uncle John's.

Again, there was no welcoming leap from Tiny. I called to my uncle. There was no answer. I entered the shack. It was empty. From the far end of the living room, the great Sioux holy bird woven into the central mat stared at me through arrowhead eyes.

I was overcome by absolute exhaustion. The nausea returned. There was nothing in my belly. As my knees began to buckle, I stumbled toward Uncle John's tiny bedroom, collapsed on the single bed covered with a log cabin patterned quilt and fell into a dream-haunted sleep.

I lay in a heap on Shaman's Point. Below, the Indian boy struggled up the steep path toward me. The great holy bird from the mat swooped down, grasped me in its talons and began to spiral straight up toward the sun. Higher and higher it flew. The small boy had reached the point of the rock and stood with his arms outstretched.

The bird released me. I drifted slowly downward toward the waiting boy. He was in danger from my falling body. I screamed, "Get out of the way! Let me die alone!"

The boy continued to reach—and smile.

I struck his arms. My momentum carried us off Shaman's Point. We embraced each other.

At the moment we were about to strike the jagged rocks below I was shocked awake by a rough, warmly moist sensation on my left cheek. Tiny had leaped on the bed and was licking me awake.

Uncle John chuckled in the background, encouraging the dog: "That's it, T-T-Tiny. Get him. Get him up. Get that lazy kid out of our bed."

Groggily, I lifted my head off the pillow. The room and its occupants were whirling. Tiny shifted her attention to my forehead. The world came into gradual focus.

Uncle John continued, "Listen here, boy—don't you have a home of your own? I came in yesterday, and it looked to me like you and that old fish friend of ours m-m-must have had a real feast out of the bread drawer. I didn't even go down yesterday evening. If I gave him any more, he might founder!

"I b-b-baked some more this morning. It's almost seven o'clock at night. If you're through with your beauty sleep, let's go down and see our finny friend."

I tried to stop him. "W-W-W-W-W"—but the word "wait" would not come.

He moved to the bread drawer and took out an extra large loaf of beautiful fresh bread. He was smiling in anticipation of his favorite part of the day.

Tiny had led him halfway down the path before my rubbery legs carried me shakily to the door.

As I stepped through the bushes onto the launching rock, I was oblivious to the foot-lacerating ridges. Uncle John had laid the bread on the rock and was staring into the west. Blood-red light from the lowering sun set the whole area afire. The distant windows of the little Baptist Church of Peter-the-Rock were blazing rubies.

Breaking his reverie, Uncle John turned, knelt and slapped

the water three times. I stood rigid, observing as if I were an outcropping of the rock itself.

After waiting a few moments, Uncle John slapped the water again—this time with more urgency.

He turned to me. For the first time in weeks he stammered within these sacred precincts.

"I-I-I'm a l-l-l-little w-w-worried. The old gr-gr-grubber f-f-fish d-doesn't s-s-seem to be c-c-coming tonight. I h-h-hope n-n-nothing's h-h-happened to him."

Tears diamonding on his cheeks caught the blood-red rays. At that moment I realized more fully than before just what the grubber fish meant to the lonely, kneeling man. I thought there were no more tears left within me. Sobs came.

He didn't rise. Looking at me strangely, he knelt there.

Finally he stammered out, "R-R-R-Rog, d-d-do y-y-you kn-know something ab-about the gr-gr-grubber f-f-fish?"

I sobbed out the whole shameful tale, my flailing tongue struggling to shape the words.

For a long time he stared at me in disbelief. His glance swept across the surface of the rock.

I knew what he was going to do. The oak cudgel used to kill the King of the Holy Lake lay where George had dropped it. Uncle John would pick it up and give me the only beating I had ever fully deserved. He would drub out my despair. I would welcome that. Let the blows reshape me into a boy worthy of the love of the man and the great fish.

He rose in slow motion and moved toward me. He paused at the cudgel, picked it up, turned toward the lake and threw it far out onto the water.

He continued toward me, sobbing as he came. His arms opened. I rushed into them. We encircled each other.

In the distance a mourning dove's call predicted rain. Maybe the violence of a sudden storm might take us both away so we could really join our invisible friends on Shaman's Point.

Our sobs subsided. He took me firmly by the shoulders in a grip which cut into my soft flesh. He looked at me deeply and said, with no trace of a stammer: "Rog, don't you ever again try to buy a friend. Don't ever try to buy a friend with money or your body or with anything else. When you do, something always dies in the process—something inside you, or something outside like my best friend in the whole world. Sometimes they both die together."

He folded me in his arms again and held me close in love so that I could truly begin to understand what he had said.

He dropped his arms and stepped out of my embrace.

"Well," he said, "I guess we might as well eat."

The sunlight had changed to burnished gold. My Hermit Uncle John picked up the bread, turned to the west, losing himself for a moment in the beauty, and lifted the bread as if to gain a benediction from the dying day. He broke it and handed half to me.

While we ate, he put an arm around me to ward off the evening chill descending on the fast-darkening world. As we finished the bread, a white gull landed on the floating cudgel. She rode it until darkness fell and we could see no more. Every iota of nausea had disappeared.

He knelt at the crystal spring, cupped his hands tightly, filled them and offered me a drink. I took his cupped hands and guided them to my lips with more gentleness and respect than if they'd been a silver chalice. I drank it all.

He knelt again, cupped his huge hands, filled them with water and stood up. He held his hands above my head and let the icy liquid drench my hair, cascade down my back and chest, between my buttocks, around my loins and down my legs. After twenty-four hours of desperation, I felt alive again.

Yet a third time he knelt and filled his cupped hands. Rising, he turned toward the west. The fading sky flared for a moment's arabesque of red and silver. Shaman's Point caught fire. I looked at the man silhouetted in the fading glow. His hands were raised to his lips. At that moment, to me, my Hermit Uncle John was again six-foot-four.

Dear Gletha,

I think I growed up tonight. I haven't written you for a long time because I've been feeling the worst about myself I ever felt. I won't tell you all the terrible things I did, but I really hurt my Hermit Uncle John.

And you know what he did tonight? He forgave me and taught me and fed me right there on the shore of the holy lake.

Right now I feel about the best about myself I ever felt.

I just wanted you to know.

Love,

Roger

Dear Roger,

The last letter from you was the best letter I ever read. It sounds to me like you met the living Jesus. If not him, then it's somebody pretty close to him.
I'm glad.

Love,

Gletha

P. S. I hope you noticed how I began this letter "Dear Roger" in honor of my growed-up boy.